The Dream Team of 1947

The
Dream Team
of 1947

*The story of how a small Iowa college upset all the major
powers to win the NCAA Wrestling Championship in 1947*

Arno P. Niemand

Boulder, Colorado
2012

The Dream Team of 1947

Library of Congress Cataloging in Publication Data
Arno P. Neimand
TXu 1-718-467, September, 2010
ISBN: 978-0-615-41703-5

Printed in the United States of America

Dedication

For Coach Paul K. Scott, the Cornell College wrestling team of 1947
and for Richard Small '50, Merron Seron '57, and R. K Scott '63,
the keepers of the flame

"It is not the critic who counts; not the man who points out how the strong man stumbles, or where the doer of deeds could have done them better. The credit belongs to the man who is actually in the arena, whose face is marred by dust and sweat and blood; who strives valiantly; who errs, and comes short again and again, because there is no effort without error and shortcoming; but who does actually strive to do the deeds; who knows the great enthusiasms, the great devotions; who spends himself in a worthy cause; who at the best knows in the end the triumph of high achievement, and who at the worst, if he fails, at least fails while daring greatly, so that his place shall never be with those cold and timid souls who know neither victory nor defeat."

—THEODORE ROOSEVELT, *address at the Sorbonne, Paris, April 23, 1910*

Table of Contents

Preface

I came to this story quite honestly.

When I was a 14-year-old schoolboy beginning wrestling in the late fall of 1948, our wrestling coach had a shopworn copy of *Life* magazine dated February 23, 1948, in his office. Coach would point to the article on the college wrestling team that had won the National Collegiate Athletic Association (NCAA) Wrestling Championship in 1947. This, of course, was the Cornell College team of Mount Vernon, Iowa.

I later went on to wrestle at Cornell University in Ithaca, New York ("the other Cornell," as the CC people like to call it). It turned out that our coach, Jimmy Miller, had actually wrestled against Cornell College twice in 1947, once in a dual meet at Ithaca, then in the National Amateur Athletic Union (NAAU) championships in San Francisco. I did not discover that until I began research for this book.

Then in the fall of 2003, *Sports Illustrated* ran an article on Herb Brooks, coach of the famous 1980 U. S. Olympic hockey team that defeated the Russians in a legendary upset, who had died in an automobile accident. It was not so much the article itself but a letter to the editor the following week that caught my eye, for it was written by Cornell College alum Nelson "Bud" Andrus, who said, What about that tiny Cornell College team that pulled the great upset in 1947 to win the NCAA Wrestling Championship, the only private college ever to do so?

This was all too much serendipity for me, and I started to delve into this story.

First I visited Cornell College in the fall of 2003 to attend the memorial service for Paul K. Scott, the coach of that 1947 team, and to tour the beautiful campus. Then I set out to do interviews and research for a possible book. But in the course of this research, a much larger story unfolded . . . .

Introduction

The first team ever to be honored by the National Wrestling Hall of Fame was Cornell College, a small, private college in Mount Vernon, Iowa, that won the NCAA Wrestling Championship in 1947. Heretofore, only individuals—wrestlers and coaches known as "distinguished members"—had been eligible. So select is the Hall that thus far (through June 2011) only 164 individuals have been inducted in 35 years.

The celebration took place June 1, 2007, in Stillwater, Oklahoma. Several of the squad members returned for the reunion, including Richard Small of Tulsa who, with his wife Norma, presided as hosts. In attendance were two members of the starting lineup, Fred Dexter and Al Partin, and team members Ben McAdams, Lynn Styles, Ben O'Dell, Al Soper, and Joe Pelisek, along with Cornell's vice president for alumni, Terry Gibson '54, and the current coach, Mike Duroe. I was privileged to make the presentation.

The National Wrestling Hall of Fame, established as the official shrine and museum of amateur wrestling—the "Cooperstown of Wrestling"—stands at the northeast corner of the Oklahoma State (formerly Oklahoma A&M) campus in Stillwater, just a hundred yards from the Gallagher-Iba Arena. University alumni, headed by Dr. Melvin D.

1

Jones, were responsible for the Hall's creation in 1976. Bob Dellinger, one of the leading journalists and historians of the sport, served as executive director from its inception until he stepped down in 1993, and Myron W. Roderick—former Oklahoma State wrestler, coach, and athletic director—took over. It is now in the capable hands of Lee Roy Smith, also a former Oklahoma State wrestler.

The rarest prize in collegiate wrestling is the NCAA team championship. Since 1934, when teams were first officially recognized by the NCAA, only 10 teams have won the title; five are multiple winners, and five are one-time winners—including Cornell College, the only private college ever to win. Cornell was also the first college outside the state of Oklahoma to win the team championship: Oklahoma A&M had previously won every team title save one, which was won by the University of Oklahoma.

A 1997 issue of the Cornell Report features the NCAA Wrestling Championship trophy brought home by the wrestling team fifty years earlier.

In an era when there was only one division for all colleges, little Cornell College decisively defeated the reigning champions and all the other powerhouses of the postwar period in the 1947 tournament held on the campus of the University of Illinois at Champaign-Urbana. Not only did the team win that NCAA tournament, but it followed up two weeks later by winning the equally prestigious NAAU championship at the Olympic Club in San Francisco, thus being one of only two teams ever to win the "grand slam" in the postwar period.

This compelling story, framed by the Great Depression and World War II, involves a nurturing liberal arts college with high academic standards; a charismatic coach who was a larger-than-life character (although he stood only 5 feet 4 inches tall); three superstar freshman from the same Iowa high school; and five WWII veterans plus several supporting cast members, including a flamboyant team manager.

The central character of the story is Paul Scott, the extraordinary coach of this great team. At three significant periods in his life he found himself at the picturesque college in the small town of Mount Vernon, a 30-minute drive north of Iowa City and 30 minutes east of Cedar Rapids. He came first as a student/athlete (1925–29), then as a coach/athletic director (1941–50), and finally as alumni director (1954–76).

The story also includes the three major obstacles Scott confronted in his coaching career: first, the loss of eight out of his eleven "starters" to the war effort, cutting short the 1943 season; then the lack of enough experienced wrestlers to field a team in 1946, when most of his competitors were able to do so; and finally, the serious car crash involving two of his stars near the end of the 1948 season, just prior to both national championships, which Cornell College was preparing to defend, and the Olympic trials held that same year.

This unique story begins and ends with Paul Scott.

Genesis of the Dream Team

Paul Scott

Paul Kenmore Scott was born October 1, 1905, to Jesse T. and Adelia DuBois Scott in the small agricultural community of West Liberty, Iowa (population 1,500), just 38 miles from Mount Vernon. The working class family Paul grew up in included an older brother and two younger sisters.

His grandfather, whom he idolized, was a Civil War veteran and was for several years the county treasurer in the nearby city of Muscatine, on the Mississippi River. Grandfather and father also partnered in the grocery business in both towns.

Some years earlier a German immigrant, one John F. Boepple, accidentally cut his foot on what turned out to be a mussel shell and upon investigation discovered that mussels grew prolifically in beds along the bottoms of freshwater streams in the vicinity of Muscatine. In 1891 he opened the first button-making factory in the city, producing pearl buttons for shirts; others soon followed, and by 1910 Muscatine had become the center of the button-making industry.

Scott's father worked in the button manufacturing business for several years, and the family lived in Muscatine from about the time Scott was two until he was six years old. It was doubtless a great business if you were an owner, another story if you were a worker.

In 1911 a strike for better wages and working conditions resulted in a lockout, during which the manufacturers farmed out the cutting of buttons to workers in their homes. In order to break the strike, factory owners brought in a band of Chicago thugs to beat up the strike's ring leaders. Scott's father, who was in charge of the commissary where the striking families could get staple foods, had to carry a gun. It was a frightening and dangerous time, and young Scott would never forget it. His sensitivity to social injustice was to influence his politics for the rest of his life.

Inevitably, the strike was broken; one of the early attempts at unionization had failed. The family moved permanently back to West Liberty, where young Scott began first grade. For a couple years, Scott's father had a small button facility of his own in West Liberty, employing as many as six people before it folded. He eventually became a railway detective. Scott's mother was the only person on either side of his family who had finished high school.

Scott was a good student, played baseball and basketball, and worked a part-time job in a shoe store. He grew up idolizing, among other Iowans, "Farmer" Burns and his protégée Frank Gotch, the greatest professional wrestlers of their day.

Scott was also the custodian for the West Liberty Opera House, a multi-purpose building that was used for movies, stage shows, and dances. Scott would clean up the Cracker Jack and popcorn boxes and sweep the place out. The theatre seats were on skids and could be lifted up and put on the stage, thus making space for the semi-pro basketball team that played its games there. Scott especially valued the perk this provided: since he had free access to the basketballs and the court, he was able to practice "shooting hoops." Scott said, "Even though I was small, I had an advantage because I could practice all weekend, and soon I could shoot better than the average guy."

In an interview in 1997 with Darren Miller, Cornell's director of sports information, Scott said that when he graduated from high school in 1924 he thought his athletic career would be over. He was working full time in the local shoe store and did not anticipate going to college, due to financial constraints. However, as luck would have it, he was in a local restaurant one evening when several of his friends were home from college for Christmas break.

"A number of my high school buddies were going to Coe," Scott said. "But the son of the Methodist minister in town went to Cornell. The group of Coe guys said, 'Scotty, why don't you come to Coe?' But the fella from Cornell said, 'He's already decided to go to Cornell.' Those Coe guys turned on me like a pack of dogs." Coe College, located in Cedar Rapids, was a fierce rival of Cornell's in both athletic and student recruitment.

The following morning, Scott's friend from Cornell made a return visit, said he sincerely wanted him to attend Cornell, and during spring break took Scott to visit the campus in his Model T. Scott was awarded a half scholarship to the college on the basis of a newspaper clipping about the state basketball tournament he had played in. That along with the money he had earned at the shoe store would carry him through his first year. In order to save money he boarded at the home of the local Presbyterian minister in Mount Vernon.

Pivot Man

Joseph T. Meade '17 was the man who could take credit for bringing Scott to Cornell in the fall of 1925. Meade served as dean of men and helped out in admissions. Scott told Meade about the basketball and baseball he had played in high school. When asked about football, Scott fibbed and said, yes, he'd played football too. Meade asked, "What do you play?" and Scott replied, "Quarterback."

In reality, his football experience was something less: "While at West Liberty High, I'd gone up to Iowa [Iowa City] and used to hang over the board fence at the south end of the old stadium and watch Aubrey Devine, one of the famous University of Iowa football stars of the period," Scott admitted.

"Much to my consternation, when I went out for football that fall, Meade was the freshman coach. So I played for my life. Aubrey was a great pivoter, and I started doing that. I really played with intensity."

Meade recalled that Scotty made the grade as a first-string quarterback on the freshman team, and "by the time he reached varsity, he was one of the best quarterbacks we had ever had."

Cornell had dropped baseball before Scott enrolled, and his basketball career did not last long. According to Darren Miller, a chemistry lab assignment forced Scott to miss part of his opening basketball practice. While Scott was in the lab, his coach instructed the team to play a zone defense. When Scott tardily entered the game, he recalled, "I chased this guy around [in man-to-man defense] and the coach ran me out. And he yelled, 'Don't come back.'"

Scott's absence from basketball practice was apparently noticed by Dick Barker, the wrestling coach, who told him to "get his ass out for wrestling." He wrestled in the 128-pound class.

By the time he graduated with a bachelor's degree in sociology in 1929, Scott had played three varsity seasons of football and wrestling, and as a senior he was captain in both sports. Scott competed in only one national wrestling tournament, the NAAU tournament of 1927, held at Iowa State University in Ames. He was present at the first NCAA tournament ever held at Iowa State, in March 1928, but did not compete due to injury.

Dr. Raymond Clapp of Nebraska had led a successful campaign to hold the tournament at Iowa State, where his protégé Hugo Otopalik was the coach. Of the 16 colleges represented, only Oklahoma A&M and Iowa State entered full teams. Forty wrestlers in all competed. Richard W. "Dick" Barker, Cornell College coach, submitted four entrants. There was no team title, but teams from the Big Ten and the Missouri Valley (later Big Six) dominated the field. The eastern schools totally ignored the event. Oklahoma A&M clearly had the best showing, with its Canadian heavyweight Earl McCready winning the first of his three NCAA titles. Finn Eriksen, who was just beginning his wrestling career at Iowa State Teachers College, also competed in the tournament; Eriksen was destined to become one of the major figures in Iowa wrestling history.

Throughout his college days, Scott earned tuition money during the summer months. After his freshman year he worked as a crewman primarily setting up tents for Chautauqua assemblies in the Midwest. The Chautauqua Movement, which was founded in 1874 at Chautauqua Lake in southwest New York, provided summertime cultural and educational experiences for vacationing Americans. From New York the movement quickly spread westward as Tent or Circuit Chautauquas, which at their peak in the 1920s brought orators, performers, and educators to thousands of sites each summer. For about 10 days—often the highlight of their summer—townsfolk gathered under a huge tent to enjoy the offerings of the traveling circuit. Setting up the enormous tents required a lot of grunt labor, and Paul Scott loved doing it. For the next three summers he worked at the Old Faithful Lodge in Yellowstone National Park.

Scott had been advised by a college sociology professor to attend graduate school, but he had bills to pay and needed a job. After graduation in 1929, he stayed in summer school, taking extra education courses to earn a teaching certificate, and that fall followed several of his college teammates into coaching. The economic situation was grim. The stock market crashed on Tuesday, October 24, 1929—the infamous "Black Tuesday"—and the Great Depression started early in 1930; it was to last right up until World War II. It was in this environment that Paul Scott entered the labor market.

According to Art Hough, in a June 6, 1976, article in the Cedar Rapids *Gazette*, Scott got his first coaching job at the Orient (Iowa) High School on the basis of an interview at the old Randolph Hotel in Des Moines, during the Drake Relays (one of the two great track and field events of the day, along with Philadelphia's Penn Relays). The female superintendent at Orient interviewed him on the hotel's mezzanine in the presence of her missionary sister. The superintendent later told Scott that her sister had influenced her decision to give him the job, because she liked his "wit and personality."

Scott's job at Orient included coaching four sports—football, basketball, track, and baseball—plus the wrestling program he introduced. He later said, "I would stand in a doorway that separated the gym and talk with the wrestlers in one room and the basketball team in the other." His football team, "loaded with talent, clobbered everyone in that area." In fact, five of his players went on to play at Cornell College. He also taught general science, American history, modern history, physics, and junior high school physical education. "I was up until midnight every night, trying to stay ahead of the kids," he said. After two years he moved on.

From 1931 to 1935 Scott taught and coached at Creston High School and Junior College. Scott said, "The Depression was really on us then. The banks closed. I had most of my football and basketball players living in the loft above the Creston fire station. My junior college boys went around town and collected food for a soup line. They got their room free, and if they happened to be there, they'd go along to put out fires. They collected the food, did the cooking and got their meals that way." When school enrollment dropped below 70, football was dropped, to Scott's great disappointment.

Scott spent the summers of 1933 and 1934 at Columbia University

Teachers College in New York City, working toward his masters in health and physical education. He also indulged his love for jazz, frequenting the local jazz clubs as much as his time allowed. On June 21, 1934, Scott married Elizabeth Campbell of Corning, Iowa, a woman he first met while they were both teaching at Orient High School, and he received his master's degree that same summer.

The newlyweds moved to Chillicothe, Missouri, where from 1935 to 1937 Scott was director of athletics and physical education at the high school and coach of football, basketball, and track. Again, he added a wrestling program.

The Scotts then moved to Culver Stockton College, a small school in Canton, Missouri, near the Mississippi, just south of the Iowa border. He was director of athletics and physical education, and football and track coach, from 1937 to 1941. His football team shared the conference championship during his third season, then won it outright the next season. Those were the only football championships for Culver Stockton in 144 years.

The Scotts' only son, Richard, was born October 15, 1940. The young family was happy at Culver Stockton, but Scott was struggling to make ends meet. The nation was still recovering from the Great Depression, and colleges were having a tough time paying faculty. "When the banks closed, they had to cut salaries to keep personnel. I was making $1,900 and that was cut down to $1,350," said Scott.

Scott Returns

Meanwhile, back at Cornell College, things were not going well in the athletic department. A news release dated February 20, 1941, described the outcome: President John B. Magee of Cornell College announced that Dick Barker, athletic director and football, wrestling, and track coach, would "sever his connection with the college at the end of the present academic year." President Magee also announced that the recent resignation of basketball coach Judd Dean had been accepted.

According to C. William Heywood, author of *Cornell College: A Sesquicentennial History*, the relationship between Barker and Dean had deteriorated until it was so tense and hostile that it became a matter of public knowledge and a disruptive influence on the department's programs. Neither had another position at the time of his resignation. A year later, Barker accepted a position as football coach at Franklin and Marshall College in Lancaster, Pennsylvania, where his mentor, Charles W. "Uncle Charlie" Mayser, was athletic director and wrestling coach. He left after two years to take a job at Curtis Publishing Company. In 1964 he was fatally injured when a train struck his car at a grade crossing near his home outside State College, Pennsylvania.

Barker had starred in both football and wrestling at Iowa State immediately following the First World War. He was an all-American football lineman and was undefeated for two years as a 175-pound wrestler. His coach in both these sports was Mayser, "the Father of Iowa wrestling." Following graduation, Barker played professional football for one year for the Decatur Staleys, the team that later became the Chicago Bears.

Barker joined the Cornell faculty in 1922, introduced wrestling, then left at the end of that year to become head wrestling and assistant football coach at the University of Michigan. When Barker left Cornell, his coaching duties were taken over by L. A. "Polly" Wallace, his teammate at Iowa State, who served from 1923 until 1925, when Wallace became head wrestling coach at the University of Oklahoma.

When the position opened up at Cornell, Barker accepted the invitation to return in 1925 as director of athletics, head coach of wrestling, and assistant coach of football. Barker became well known as the man who introduced intercollegiate wrestling to Cornell and developed a program in the sport that won national recognition for him and the college. Indeed,

Cornell College had a man on every Olympic team from 1924 through 1956. Barker coached not only Paul Scott but also Claude Reeck, the Purdue coach, and Lloyd Appleton, the Army coach who was a two-time Olympian and a silver medalist in 1928. Barker was an "old-school," no-nonsense coach whose nickname was "Bull."

Wallace "Pic" Littell, who wrestled under both Barker and Scott, said of the two that Barker could take an Iowa farm boy and make him into an Olympian, while Scott could mold an entire team into a national champion.

Judd Dean, whose departure was announced along with Barker's, was a successful coach of basketball and track at Cornell, first from 1926 to 1931 and again from 1935 to 1941. A Cornell alumnus, class of 1926, he had played for and captained Cornell's championship football and basketball teams of 1925 and 1926. He and Scott met as Cornell students, and they remained lifelong friends. Dean served for three years in Europe in the Army Air Corps during World War II, leaving the service as a lieutenant colonel.

Dr. Glenn Cunningham, director of health services at Cornell, was named director of athletics, physical education, and health effective September 1, 1941. Cunningham was probably best known for his outstanding career as a distance runner, which included winning the prestigious Sullivan Award as the nation's outstanding amateur athlete, being a member of the 1936 Olympic team, and running the fastest mile ever in the U.S. in 1939, a record of 4:04:04.

Cunningham named Walt Koch coach of football and basketball and offered Scott the job of wrestling coach and assistant football coach, at a starting salary of $3,000 per year. Scott felt he had to take this much-higher-paying job, although he was reluctant to give up his head coaching job in football and was concerned about how his relationship with Cunningham would work out. But as Scott later put it, "We got along great. We were very good friends. He was really good to work with." Scott's decision to return was to have far-reaching consequences for Cornell College and for himself and his family.

Cornell College

Cornell College is situated on a scenic, wooded hilltop overlooking the town of Mount Vernon, which today has a population of about 3,800. Founded in 1853 by George Bryant Bowman, a Methodist minister, it was originally known as the Iowa Conference Seminary. The school was renamed in 1857 after William Wesley Cornell, a prosperous upstate New York businessman and devout Methodist who, along with his brother, gave the college modest sums of money and books. The school made the naming gesture in the hope that a major contribution would follow, which never happened; by all rights the school should have been named after Reverend Bowman. (A distant cousin of Wesley Cornell's, Ezra Cornell,

A view of Cornell College today. The campus of the school, which was founded in 1853, is listed on the National Register of Historic Places.

14

founded Cornell University in 1865.) Cornell was the first college west of the Mississippi to grant women the same rights as men, and in 1858 it was the first Iowa college to graduate a woman.

It is one of only two college campuses in the country listed on the National Register of Historic Places. Most of the main campus consists of buildings dating from the late 1800s to the early 1900s. In 1905, Cornell was the first college to be awarded a Carnegie library, under the condition that it be shared by Mount Vernon residents. It was the first building on campus constructed with steel, a requirement of the benefactor, the steel magnate Andrew Carnegie.

The school was a traditional four-year liberal arts college until 1978, when it switched to a "one-course-at-a-time" curriculum modeled after that of Colorado College in Colorado Springs. After a difficult transition, the college has once again taken its place as an outstanding liberal arts college.

When Paul Scott reported for his new job at Cornell in the fall of 1941, the student enrollment was 655, with an almost equal male–female ratio. The population of the town was 1,441. In the fall semester, Scott coached cross-country and assisted with football. Male students were encouraged to participate in as many sports as possible, and many of the heavier-weight wrestlers also played football.

The Japanese attack on Pearl Harbor on December 7, 1941, "changed the campus climate drastically" according to historian Heywood. "The draft and enlistments cut seriously into male enrollment in the college; the male–female enrollment was 322–313 in 1940/41, 59–370 in 1943/44 and 60–453 in 1944/45. The second semester of 1941/42 was shortened by cancelling spring vacation and advancing commencement from June 9 to May 18, in order to reduce travel and permit more students to complete the academic year before entering military service."

The Sport of Wrestling in the 1940s

Wrestling in those days was a blue-collar sport. Edward C. Gallagher, the famous Oklahoma A&M coach, wrote, "It is easier for the camel to pass through the eye of a needle than it is for a rich man's son to be a wrestler," and he advised coaches to "select really poor boys who cannot go out into society." While the social aspect was more than likely disputable, the working class element was not.

R. T. "Bob" Mitchell, the longtime coach at Osage (Iowa) High School, who coached the great Iowa State Teachers College wrestler Gerald "Gerry" Leeman, among others, once said of his wrestlers, "Most of them have been husky farm boys and wiry small-town boys from families of modest means." "Give me a poor kid every time," said Mitchell.

In the post-war period, high school sports were seasonal. Almost all boys played football on some level. A few of the lighter boys would run cross-country. In the winter months, basketball was the main sport. More affluent schools had swimming pools and therefore a swim team, and a few schools had wrestling. Physical education (P.E.) was mandatory for those not participating in varsity sports. In the spring there was baseball and/or track and field, if facilities were available. There were few if any sports for girls.

The self-selection process in wrestling was rigorous. Many boys did not make it through their first season, and those who lasted their entire four years considered it a major achievement. There were many brother combinations, even twins. Farm boys and ranchers' sons loved to wrestle. Supporters were mostly family and friends.

Strength training was limited and confined mostly to calisthenics and rope climbing. Cardio fitness was achieved through running and rope jumping. Nutritional education was virtually nonexistent.

In collegiate wrestling there were eight weight classes: 121, 128, 136, 145, 155, 165, 175, and heavyweight. The population was smaller in stature then, and a "big" man weighed 180 to 185 pounds and was typically between 5'10" and 5'11" tall. Wrestlers were expected to wrestle at two classes and maybe three in some instances.

Matches always began with the lightest weight class and moved up through heavyweight. This system was not changed until the 1998/99 season, when a random draw was introduced.

Wrestling matches were nine minutes long, divided into three three-minute periods. In the first period, the wrestlers began from the standing (neutral) position. The second and third periods started on the mat in the referee's position: both wrestlers were on their knees, one in the "top" position with his arm around the waist of his opponent, who was in the "bottom" position. Before the start of the second period, a coin toss by the referee determined who would choose top or bottom; the wrestlers reversed position in the next period.

If a **fall** (pin) occurred, the match was over. A fall was declared when either wrestler held his opponent's shoulder to the mat for a period of two seconds.

In a match in which a fall did not occur, the winner was determined by a point scoring system:

Takedown (taking the opponent to the mat with advantage): two points.

Escape (escaping from the opponent's advantage and gaining a starting position): one point.

Reversing position, or reversal (escaping from opponent's advantage and gaining advantage): two points.

Near fall (holding the opponent's shoulders to the mat for less than two seconds or holding opponent's shoulders near the mat for two seconds or more): three points.

True advantage or "riding time" (holding a position of advantage over opponent for one minute or more longer than he has advantage over you): one point. Holding a two-minute time advantage earned two points.

In the case of a draw at the end of nine minutes, two two-minute overtime periods were wrestled. If those also resulted in a tie, the match was a draw. In tournaments, however, the referee decided the outcome of a draw in what was called a referee's decision. There were no set criteria for this decision, and usually it was based on the judgment of which wrestler was more aggressive. The decision was very often awarded to a defending champion. Needless to say, the process was rather arbitrary and often controversial.

This point scoring system was introduced officially by the NCAA in 1941, although schools and colleges had been using it since the late 1930s. Before that, bouts were decided by a fall, riding time, or referee's decision.

The outcome of each individual match contributed to the team score: a fall was worth five points; a decision, three points; and in case of a draw, each team was awarded two points.

Scott's First Season

Scott began his first season as Cornell's head wrestling coach with no college coaching experience (he had, however, initiated programs at two of the high schools where he coached, for two seasons each). He inherited a team from Barker that included Frank Preston, Wallace "Pic" Littell, Arlo Ellison, Walt Haloupek, Fred Bishop, and Dale Thomas. He also had some promising freshmen. The team's record for the season in dual-meet competition was 7 wins and 2 losses (to Illinois and Minnesota).

Dale Thomas was a farm boy from Marion, Iowa. He was an outstanding football player who had never wrestled in high school. As was customary, all the athletes lined up to meet their new coach. As Scott remembered, "Thomas had all his hair trimmed. Cut off with clippers. And I looked over and thought to myself, there's nothing but trouble here.

It started out that way, but I managed to straighten him out."

It turned out that Thomas had worries, and he confided in Scott. Thomas's father was having a circulation problem with one of his legs, and the doctor had prescribed that he take a good shot of whiskey every night before going to bed. Thomas was concerned that "they were going to make a drunkard out of his old man." Scott assured him that the doctor knew what he was doing. After that, Scott said Thomas kind of adopted him as a surrogate parent, and they got along famously. They were to remain lifelong friends.

However, Scott remembered an incident during that first 1941/42 season when Thomas proved to be a little too stubborn. Cornell was wrestling the Davenport YMCA, and Scott warned Thomas to be very careful with his opponent, Fred Dexter, whom Scott had observed previously while refereeing one of his matches. Nevertheless, Thomas took Dexter much too lightly. A great "leg wrestler," Dexter defeated Thomas badly by "scissoring him and putting him in a long half nelson," as Scott put it. When Thomas was through, he had been so stretched out that "he was about three inches taller." Dexter would defeat Thomas again that season. The following year, Thomas would even the score by defeating Dexter twice. Scott, meanwhile, was thinking that Dexter might be an excellent addition to the team.

Scott took six of his starters to Michigan State (in East Lansing, Michigan) to compete in the NCAA Tournament. (Barker had taken five men to the tournament the year before, where Fred Bishop and Walt Haloupek both gained valuable experience.) The only wrestler to place was Bishop, who took second to Bill Maxwell (Michigan State) at 136 pounds. Arlo Ellison wrestled well but was injured in his quarter-final match against the great Dave Arndt (Oklahoma A&M) and had to default in the consolation round to Newt Copple (Nebraska), whom he had defeated in their dual meet. In the 165-pound class, Dale Thomas lost to the eventual third-place finisher, William Courtright (Michigan), 3–2.

Because of the war, 1942 was the last year for the NCAA championship until 1946. The National AAU tournament, however, continued be held throughout the war years.

The 1942/43 Season

With all his key starters returning, Scott was anticipating a strong 1942/43 season, and he was not disappointed. The squad went 8-0, including wins over Iowa State and Minnesota in an abbreviated season that ended on February 13, 1943. (One of the later meets that had to be cancelled was with Iowa State Teachers College.) The Army Air Corps Reserve call abruptly ended what might have been a great post-season; as Scott put it, he lost 8 of his 11 starters to the service. Scott could have ended the season right there, but instead he elected to keep as many men working out as possible in anticipation of the NAAU meet, which was to be held April 9–10 at the West Side YMCA in New York City.

The National AAU Championship was held every year, usually in the first or second week of April, two weeks after the NCAA championship. The rules and scoring system were essentially the same as those of the collegiate system, except that final matches were 12 minutes long (three four-minute periods) and there were two additional weight classes—115 pounds and 191 pounds. The caliber of competition was on a par with the collegiate meet and consisted of the hard-core AAU types who typically wrestled for YMCAs or private clubs; many were ex-collegians, plus collegians whose coach would allow them to enter. Promising high school boys also participated, particularly in the lower weight classes, and gained valuable experience. Indeed, it was not unusual for a high school entrant to win one of the lighter weight classes. Gerry Leeman, for example, won the NAAU in 1940 at 121 pounds when he was just a junior at Osage (Iowa) High School. More unusual was the case of Joe Scarpello, a high school senior from Omaha, who won the 1942 NAAU at 165 pounds.

Scott decided to take his three remaining starters—Frank Preston, a 121-pounder who would drop to 115; Dale Thomas, 175 pounds; and Walter Haloupek, 191 pounds—plus Charlie Maguire, 165 pounds. Preston, Thomas, and Haloupek had all won state AAU titles previously. They trained for the event for five weeks, often at night, because by then the gym was shared with a military training program based on campus. The team left on a Monday by car and arrived in New York City by midweek. En route they stopped one night at Wooster College in Ohio, where the team worked out.

Attendance at the championship was of course dependent on where it was held. This year, however, there was a record number in the tournament due both to the cancellation of the NCAA championship and the addition of the many men entering from various military units. Despite wartime conditions, the tournament drew 140 entrants and was the most successful in its history, according to Dan Ferris, national secretary of the AAU. Besides the collegiate conferences that continued to function during the war years (mainly the Eastern Intercollegiate Wrestling Association and the Big Ten), the NAAU tournament was the glue that held amateur wrestling together until peacetime returned.

Although the meet was a two-day event, certain weight classes with fewer entries were held only on the second day, including those wrestled by Preston, Thomas, and Haloupek. Since Maguire was eliminated in the first round on Friday, Scott had an opportunity to observe several key bouts that day, including those of a high school senior from Newton (New Jersey) High School named Rodger Snook.

Snook, a two-time New Jersey State champion, was wrestling for the Newton Boy's Club in the 145-pound weight class. His coach and mentor was Henry Boresch, who pioneered New Jersey wrestling. Boresch's teams dominated wrestling in the state from the 1920s to the

1960s. From 1927 to 1963 he produced 66 state champions and won nine team titles. His record for dual meets for that period was 100–22–6. His wrestlers did well at Penn State, Toledo, Rutgers, Lehigh, and Franklin and Marshall, according to wrestling historian Jamie Moffatt.

Snook was wrestling a man named Jack Foster, who had gone to Purdue. Scott had seen Foster pin Fred Bishop a year ago. Scott said, "I'm watching this high school kid and I thought to myself, boy you'll wish you stayed home. This guy Foster will kill him. So Foster takes him down and rides him for the first three minutes. The second period Snook reverses Foster and pins him with a cradle." Apparently this feat went unnoticed by the other coaches, but Scott took Snook aside to congratulate him and said, "What's your plan for college, Rodger?" And he said, "Well, I would like to go to a good midwestern school, preferably a small college that has a good wrestling team." To which Scott replied, "Well, you are talking to the right man," and described the situation at Cornell College. Snook said, "Coach, I am going into the service soon, if I make it through the war, please look me up." This conversation would not be their last.

Snook proceeded to pin another opponent before being eliminated by the veteran Doug Lee (Baltimore YMCA).

According to Rodger's niece, Jane Snook Sattelberg, "Rodger had been drafted earlier but received a waiver to finish high school. After graduation he joined his three brothers and two brothers-in-law in the service. He served as an aircraft mechanic during the war."

On Saturday, Preston won three bouts to take the 115-pound title, and Thomas won four bouts within an eight-hour span to win at 175 pounds. At 191 pounds, Haloupek pinned his first-round opponent in 16 seconds; he advanced to the final, only to be pinned by the renowned Henry Wittenberg (West Side YMCA).

Scott also took note of several other wrestlers in the tournament, including three-time Eastern Intercollegiate Wrestling Association (EIWA) champion Charles Ridenour (Penn State), who won the 128-pound weight class, and Jimmy Miller (Cornell University) at 145 pounds, who lost in the finals to former NCAA champion Bill Maxwell (Michigan State).

The Cornell College team tied for second place with Michigan State, a remarkable showing considering it had only four men. The West Side YMCA won the team title.

Charles Maguire recalled that the four of them recognized that the officials and others treated Scott with respect. They were also aware that their coach was trying to make this send-off trip a special experience for them. "Scott knew all of us were destined for service and made a distinct effort to make trip sidelights memorable, besides the thrill of national competition." That tournament was one of the high points in Scott's career and in Cornell College history, but it was also bittersweet, since all the boys were departing for the various services.

Before World War II was over, 1,037 Cornellians saw service, including 75 women and 5 faculty and staff. Approximately one quarter of those who served were still students when they entered the service; the rest were alumni. Thirty-four men died in service.

Scott lost two members of the 1943 team. One was Donald F. Fish '43, a fighter pilot who was shot down in the Pacific. The other casualty was one of those four men Scott took to the NAAU, starter Walter D. Haloupek '43, from Belle Plaine, Iowa, who was not only an outstanding athlete but an excellent scholar. He majored in physics, was named to Phi Beta Kappa, and served as class president in both his junior and senior years. After graduation, he received his military training at the U.S. Naval Academy, after which he remained at Annapolis as an instructor. He was recruited by the Washington Redskins and played for them against the College All-Stars in the Chicago *Tribune* charity game in August 1943. He then applied for and was granted permission to transfer to the submarine service. Navy Ensign Haloupek was lost at sea on his first trip out, when his submarine the USS *Harder* (SS-257) was sunk by surface craft on August 24, 1944; all seventy-nine men aboard were lost.

Scott took these losses very hard, and he was always frustrated by the fact that he himself was not eligible to serve, due to a combination of factors—his age, height, marital status, and fatherhood.

In the summer of 1943, Scott withdrew from coaching to join the Cornell admissions staff. He traveled throughout the Midwest, primarily in Iowa and Illinois, to interview and recruit prospective students, both male and female. Gasoline rationing was in effect, and gasoline was 15 cents per gallon; the speed limit was 35 m.p.h.

In the winter months he also refereed high school wrestling matches in eastern Iowa, making his presence known in the wrestling community and, of course, scouting for talent. Refereeing required a complete knowledge of the rules, impartiality, energy, and the willingness to sacrifice being away from home a certain number of nights. Scott would continue to do this during his entire tenure at the college and was one of the most highly regarded referees in the state, along with Finn Eriksen, Hugh Linn, and Fred Cooper. The compensation for a referee was usually $20 per meet.

It was not, however, all work and no play, as can be seen in a letter written by Norma Morrissey, the wife of Al Morrissey, a friend of Scott's who owned an insurance agency in Mount Vernon: "I rode to Davenport with Scotty and Bess last night. He refereed a wrestling meet. We had a good time. He was paid $20, and I doubt if he was able to account for much of it when he got home. He made me think of Tim when he gets a little money in his pockets. We drank, ate, chewed, smoked. He bought a bottle of liquor to take home, bought Betty a bottle of cologne, Rich a box of candy. He's so cute. We very nearly froze on the way home. The heater didn't heat at all, and last night was one of the coldest we've had. We each had a blanket around our legs, but my feet were numb. I said it last winter and I'll say it again – 'I'll never go through another winter without stadium boots!'"

The War Effort Comes to Campus

With enrollment and tuition income declining due to the draft and enlistments, colleges and universities nationwide faced serious financial problems, according to Heywood. Cornell College was no exception. "At the same time," he wrote, "the government needed more military training programs than could be accommodated at traditional bases."

President Magee moved quickly in November 1942 to present Cornell's case to the War Department, and the college was chosen as a site for one of twenty Naval Flight Preparatory Schools (NFPS). Operations began in January 1943 with 200 men arriving at overlapping intervals of three months, for a total of 600 men at any given time. That original program was later replaced by a Naval Academic Refresher Unit (NARU), which remained on campus until January 1946. Altogether, 4,000 naval trainees went through the two programs. Jimmy Miller of Cornell University, whom Scott had first encountered in New York in 1943, was one of those Mount Vernon trainees. During this period the college arranged for some female students and all the regular male students to live in private homes in town.

The naval training programs saved the college financially. By the time the last of the units departed at the end of the war, Cornell's enrollment of regular students was rising rapidly due to the influx of returning veterans, aided by the GI Bill.

The GI Bill and the Post-war Period

Many government and business leaders feared that massive unemployment would follow WWII, so as early as 1942 planners had looked ahead to preparing America for peacetime. The GI Bill, officially designated "The

Servicemen's Readjustment Act," was passed by Congress and signed into law by President Franklin Roosevelt on June 22, 1944.

Of a veteran population of 15.4 million, more than half, 7.8 million, took advantage of the opportunities offered by this innovative piece of legislation: job training, loans for housing, and tuition assistance, along with unemployment compensation. The influx of veterans into the university system was huge enough—the number of college graduates between 1940 and 1950 more than doubled—to create a knowledge society in America. Likewise, the flood of new home owners resulted in the creation of suburbs. Stephen Ambrose, noted author-historian, called the GI Bill "the best piece of legislation ever passed by the U.S. Congress and it made modern America."

On the Cornell Campus specifically, the GI Bill enabled veterans to matriculate at this small, private college with the same level of financial aid that a full scholarship would have provided at a larger university. In other words, for a brief period, the government tuition aid leveled the playing field.

The optimism and opportunity embodied in the GI Bill captured the mood of a country that had just emerged victorious from the cataclysm of World War II. David Halberstam quoted the sportscaster Curt Gowdy, reflecting on his early days in broadcasting during that post-war period: "It was the last moment of innocence in American life."

America was a nation defined by the railroad. Passenger train service was a common means of public transport, as was travel by bus. Air travel was in its infancy. The automobile was becoming popular, in spite of the fact that no interstate highway system yet existed.

News was provided mainly by newspapers. There was at least one newspaper being published daily in almost every town in America, and all the larger cities supported several competing newspapers. Sports scores were transmitted to those papers by telegraph service.

Baseball was the national pastime. With the exception of the rare heavyweight fight or college football game that attracted national attention, baseball dominated America's sports scene.

In 1947, the year at the heart of this story, average wages per year were $2,850, and the average cost of a new car was $1,300. The average cost of a home was $1,824. Postage stamps were three cents, and at movie theatres feature films cost half a dollar. On June 5 of that year Secretary of State George C. Marshall announced the Marshall Plan for the reconstruction of Europe, and on October 14 Major Charles E. "Chuck" Yeager of the U. S. Air Force broke the sound barrier for the first time. The entire nation was focused on moving forward, getting on with life, and making the war years part of history.

A Man with a Plan

Cornell's athletic director, Glenn Cunningham, was inducted into the Navy on April 11, 1944, and was stationed at the Great Lakes Naval Training Station as an apprentice seaman. In the fall of 1945, it was announced that he would not be returning, and Russell Cole, then president of Cornell College, announced that Paul Scott would succeed him as director of physical education and intercollegiate athletics, while retaining his other duties coaching cross-country, wrestling, and track. Walt Koch remained in charge of football and basketball.

Scott now had the job he really wanted. World War II had ended officially with the Japanese surrender on August 14, 1945, and men were coming back from the service at a rapid rate. Nevertheless, Cornell College began the fall semester with about 600 students, only one third of whom were men.

Koch was able to field a respectable football team, and Scott had a successful cross-country team. The winter season saw Koch play a competitive schedule in basketball, while Scott prepared his men for the

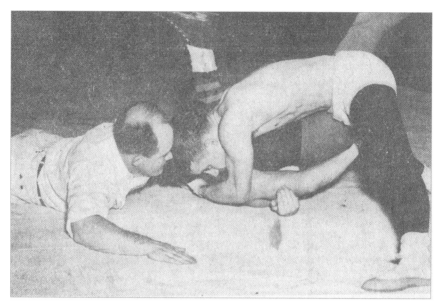

Paul Scott referees a dual meet between Teachers College and Iowa State in February 1946.

spring track season. Scott's dilemma was the wrestling program, in which both he and the school took great pride.

Wrestling season typically began after Thanksgiving, when the football and cross-country seasons were over. Scott had barely enough men available for practice sessions, let alone field a team for the collegiate season. He had only two men with any experience working out: Bob Conner, 121 pounds, who had been at Cornell for two years before joining the Navy in '43, and Jack Haloupek, heavyweight, younger brother of the late Walter Haloupek. So desperate were they for "warm bodies" that young Haloupek sent out an urgent plea for some "big men" to give him a workout.

Although both the EIWA Conference and the Big Ten, as well as some of the Big Six schools and major independents such as Iowa State Teachers College and Michigan State, were able to organize at least partial dual meet seasons in 1945/46, a few schools, including Cornell College, the University of Oklahoma, and Kansas State, were unable to do so.

Meanwhile, Scott busied himself refereeing high school matches in the eastern part of the state. Iowa State Teachers College (henceforth also referred to as "Iowa Teachers" or "Teachers"), coached by Dave McCuskey, had resumed wrestling, so Scott, who was on friendly terms with McCuskey, also refereed Iowa Teachers home meets in Cedar Falls, against Nebraska and later against Iowa State. Teachers won both team meets easily. This experience gave Scott valuable insight into what he would be up against the following year.

Scott made the rather optimistic announcement in early February that in April he would be taking a few men to the NAAU tournament in New York City, the same meet at which he had had such success with his four remaining wrestlers in 1943. Selections would be made on the basis of performances at the annual Waterloo YMCA tournament, to be held the first week in March, and at the Iowa State AAU tournament, whose status remained in doubt. These meets represented the only opportunities for open competition, and in the end, the state AAU tournament was never held.

Clarion Call

The Iowa State High School Wrestling Championship, which began in 1921, took place on February 22–23, 1946, at Clarion (Iowa) High School. Clarion hosted the championship every year from 1941 through 1947, with the exception of 1942, when it was held in Waterloo. Paul Scott was one of four officials.

Clarion was located in the north-central part of the state, due north of Des Moines and Ames. Several of the leading wrestling high schools were in that area, notably Fort Dodge, Eagle Grove, Osage, Cresco, and Clarion. Twenty-two teams from as far away as Davenport and Cherokee descended on the town, along with family and friends who stayed overnight at the hotel in downtown Clarion. A record crowd of 1,500 was in attendance for the finals. (Today, the Iowa State High School

Championship is a four-day event held at the new Wells Fargo arena in Des Moines. In 2008 more than 200 teams participated, and crowds averaged more than 15,000 per session, according to the Des Moines *Register*.)

The West Waterloo Wahawks were the four-time defending champions, coached in their first two championship seasons by the legendary Finn Eriksen before he went into the service, and for the last two by his successor, Roy Jarrard, who had won previously while the coach at Cherokee. Buses chartered by Waterloo wrestling fans left for Clarion on Saturday morning at 10 A.M. No team had ever won five straight championships, and West Waterloo would get plenty of competition from Osage, Eagle Grove, and Fort Dodge. In fact, Osage had narrowly defeated the Wahawks in the district tournament.

The Wahawks had three defending champions, all seniors—Dick Hauser, Leo Thomsen, and Lowell Lange. The team had had a long season. In addition to eight dual meets, they had participated in the Mississippi Valley Conference meet, the Big Seven Conference, and the district tournament. They lost two dual meets when Jarrard "sat" his star trio for disciplinary reasons, or "acting up" as Lowell Lange put it (who also said it was the right thing for the coach to do).

The two-day meet began with preliminaries on Friday at 7:30 P.M. and ended with the finals on Saturday at 7:30 P.M. There was only one division, and there were 10 weight classes, from 95 pounds to 155 pounds, plus heavyweight.

West Waterloo won its record-breaking fifth straight title by scoring 20 points. Clarion, Eagle Grove, and Osage schools shared runner-up honors, each team scoring 15 points. Dick Hauser won his third consecutive championship, Leo Thomsen and Lowell Lange, their second.

Scott was hoping to convince at least a couple of the newly crowned senior winners to apply to Cornell. This would not be easy. Several other prominent coaches were in attendance, including Dave McCuskey, who sat next to Lowell Lange's dad for much of the tournament. West Waterloo was only seven miles from the campus at Cedar Falls, so it would seem only natural for the Wahawk trio to attend Teachers, as many other Waterloo wrestlers had done. However, McCuskey had not expressed any interest in Hauser or Thomsen, because he had their weight classes covered.

Scott had a distinct recruiting disadvantage because Cornell College was a small private institution, with higher academic standards than those of his competitors, the large public institutions such as the University of Iowa, Iowa State, and Iowa Teachers. Scott, however, offered something unique: he let it be known to the trio from West Waterloo, plus the other senior winners, that he was planning to take some men to the National AAU Championship in New York City in April, depending on the results of the upcoming YMCA and State AAU tournaments.

Bob Conner and Jack Haloupek entered the annual Waterloo YMCA tournament in early March and both had mixed results. Conner at 120 pounds won his first match by default and then lost a close match in the finals. At heavyweight, Haloupek pinned his first opponent and was then promptly pinned himself. Not exactly the results Scott was looking for. A short time later Scott made his decision. In order to justify the trip to New York, he would take Conner, his best wrestler, and move him to the 115-pound class, where he would have a better chance of winning.

Scott met with the parents of Hauser, Thomsen, and Lange at Mr. Hauser's restaurant in Waterloo, which he frequented from time to time. He had gotten to know each of them through refereeing many team matches. He told them he would be willing to drive their boys to New York for the NAAU meet in April if they were interested, and "their parents jumped at the chance," according to Scott. He also invited two other state champions, Harry Horn of Osage and Curt Stein of Gilmore City.

The First Post-war NCAA Championship

Kenneth L. "Tug" Wilson, NCAA Secretary, had announced on February 23 that the 1946 NCAA wrestling championship would be held at Oklahoma A&M in Stillwater, Oklahoma, on March 22–23. It was last held in 1942, when the Aggies won.

According to wrestling historian Jay Hammond, the NCAA did not intend to resume the championship in 1946 but changed its mind when Oklahoma A&M offered to host the tournament. The NCAA committee relented, following a letter-writing campaign initiated by the Oklahoma A&M coach, Art Griffith. However, the short notice of only one month meant that participation was limited mainly to schools from the Midwest, inasmuch as the EIWA had stopped wrestling several weeks earlier. (Penn State was to send one man.) Indeed, only 17 schools entered 54 wrestlers, the smallest participation since the event was first held in 1928. Almost all of the coaches who brought individuals were protégées of the late Ed Gallagher, Griffith's predecessor and a legend in the history of wrestling.

Collegiate wrestling began at Ivy League colleges on the East Coast just after the turn of the 19th century. It quickly moved west to places such as the University of Nebraska at Lincoln and Iowa State University at Ames, and eventually the sport's center of gravity shifted to Stillwater, Oklahoma, home of Oklahoma A&M, where one Edward C. Gallagher held forth.

Gallagher graduated from Oklahoma A&M in 1909 with a degree in electrical engineering. He starred in football and track, but wrestling was not offered in those days. After leaving the university for a few years he returned in 1915 to become director of athletics and physical education. The next year he also became the coach of wrestling, which had just been introduced at the school. Because of WWI, few meets were held until 1920, when wrestling resumed in earnest and Gallagher proceeded to establish a record that is as impressive as any in sports history.

In his 23 years at Oklahoma A&M, 19 of his teams went undefeated. He compiled a dual meet record of 138 wins, 5 defeats, and 4 ties, and in his last 19 seasons he had only two losses. His team competed in 13 NCAA championships, winning eight official and three unofficial titles with a 95 percent winning percentage. He produced 37 NCAA champions, 15 Olympians, and 3 Olympic champions. From 1921 to 1932 his team won 68 consecutive dual meets.

Gallagher's approach to wrestling was uniquely analytical, and coaches came from near and far to learn from the man who was affectionately called the Old Master. Some of his wrestlers became the leading high school coaches in Oklahoma, while others headed up many of the country's most successful college programs, including Cliff Keen at Michigan, Paul Keen at Oklahoma, Fendley Collins at Michigan State, Rex Perry at Pittsburgh, and Ray Swartz at Navy. The man who created this remarkable dynasty died of Parkinson's Disease on August 28, 1940.

Gallagher's hand-picked successor, Art Griffith, took over in 1941 and proved to be his most outstanding protégé. Griffith had been the coach at Tulsa Central High School, the most successful high school in the history of wrestling: from 1928 to 1940 his team won 10 state championships, with 94 dual meet victories in 100 meets; 15 graduates won a total of 25 NCAA titles.

In Griffith's first two years as the Oklahoma A&M coach, his team won the NCAA championship twice, beating Michigan State 39–26 in 1941 and 31–26 in 1942. Wrestling writer Roger Moore, speaking of Griffith, said, "Incredibly, he coached ten of the sixteen NCAA finalists in 1942 in either college or high school." Now, as the NCAA championship was resuming after the hiatus of the war years, Griffith was to face a serious challenge from a new quarter: Iowa.

Scott decided to attend the tournament, driving the 1,300-mile round trip to Stillwater. Oklahoma A&M of course entered a complete team, and Iowa Teachers, coached by McCuskey, entered five wrestlers. Joining Scott in Stillwater were Finn Eriksen, who had returned from the service as the director of health and physical education for the Waterloo public school system, and Hugo Otopalik of Iowa State, considered the "dean of Iowa wrestling coaches" by Eriksen.

David B. "Buddy" Arndt, whom Art Griffith said was "the best wrestler he ever coached," came back to win his third title. George Dorsch also won for A&M at 175 pounds. Iowa Teachers had three winners in Cecil Mott (121 pounds), Gerry Leeman (128 pounds), and Bill Koll (145 pounds), the most of any school.

Arndt and Koll had both seen combat in the war. Arndt served three years as a P-38 fighter pilot, flying more than 100 combat missions over Italy, for which he was awarded the Distinguished Flying Cross and six bronze battle stars. Koll, who served for three years with the combat engineers, landed at Omaha Beach and was involved in the Battle of the Bulge, receiving a bronze star for his efforts.

Oklahoma A&M defeated Iowa Teachers by the narrowest of margins, 25–24, and only after one of the Iowa Teachers stars, Leon Martin, had been declared ineligible. This loss marked the beginning of what wrestling historian Jay Hammond has called "the Teachers' curse," which lasted until 1950, when they finally won the NCAA championship. It also marked the beginning of a shift in the balance of power in collegiate wrestling that would not be completely understood until the following year.

The Martin Incident

A week before the Iowa Teachers team was due to depart for Stillwater, its athletic director, L. L. Mendenhall, and wrestling coach, Dave McCuskey, were anxiously awaiting a decision from the NCAA regarding Leon "Champ" Martin. He had placed second in the last NCAA tournament in 1942 at 175 pounds, losing a 5–5 referee's decision to Dick DiBatista (University of Pennsylvania). Martin, who had graduated under a special wartime program, was a graduate student but had been ruled eligible for intercollegiate competition by the Big Ten, under whose athletic code Iowa Teachers operated: all registered students would be allowed to participate that season even if they held college degrees. Apparently someone had protested to the NCAA, probably the Oklahoma A&M coach Art Griffith.

The ruling had to be passed on by Kenneth "Tug" Wilson, the secretary of the NCAA. Wilson, who was also the Big Ten Commissioner, had the unenviable task of notifying Teachers that the NCAA wrestling rules committee had determined that Martin would not be eligible on the basis of his having completed his undergraduate requirements. Thus Martin had to stay home. Teachers would likely have won the team title, since Martin would certainly have scored some points. This ruling did not go down well with the Iowa crowd and is remembered to this day.

Finn Eriksen reported to the Waterloo *Courier* that "Iowa was well represented at the NCAA tournament, coming away with three of the four trophies including Leeman's Outstanding Wrestler Award and Koll's Trophy for the Fastest Fall."

Illinois finished a strong third and requested that the 1947 championship be held in Champaign-Urbana, since the school believed it might be able to win the tournament.

Scott had a lot to think about on the trip back from Stillwater, particularly the success of Iowa Teachers. Scott would always be at a disadvantage competing against the large public institutions with their bigger enrollments. However, at this moment in time there were currently two factors in operation that were to prove beneficial. The first was the GI Bill, which provided the equivalent of a full college scholarship to any man who had served in the military. (Each of Teachers' three NCAA champions were on the GI Bill.) The other key factor was the lifting of "the freshman rule." In order to give colleges a better chance to field teams during the war, the NCAA had suspended its ban on freshman eligibility from 1943 to 1947, thus allowing freshmen to participate on varsity teams. Scott had one more year to take advantage of this situation: all freshman recruits for the 1947 season would be eligible for four years of competition.

Paul Scott's Excellent Adventure

The NAAU-bound wrestlers (Bob Conner, Dick Hauser, Lowell Lange, Leo Thomsen, Harry Horn, and Curt Stein) all rendezvoused in Mount Vernon early in the week of April 10. Hauser and Thomsen had been working out, but Lange said that he had hardly worked out at all, since he was concentrating on track during the spring.

Scott had somehow confiscated an oversized 1943 International station wagon, which was salvaged from the junk pile of the Navy preflight program that had ended that year. At best it was a not-so-gently-used castoff with engine problems, but it could easily hold the six wrestlers plus the driver. They successfully made the trip to New York, staying in inexpensive rooms along the way.

There were 148 entrants in the 1946 NAAU tournament, a large field for a two-day event. Conner won two matches then lost a tough 10–6 bout to Arlie Curry, a high school senior from Tulsa who went on to win. He came back to take third place.

Hauser (121) had a tough semi-final bout against one of the Newton, New Jersey, boys, but won 9–7; he then won in the finals by default from an injured Dale Nelson, another Iowa high schooler.

The 128-pound class was loaded with talent, and in the quarter-final round Thomsen lost to Charles Ridenour (New York Athletic Club) 8–4. Ridenour was beaten in the finals by the veteran Ed Collins, also of the NYAC.

In the 136-pound class Lowell Lange handily defeated all his

Ready to hit the road: Coach Scott and the high school wrestlers he took to New York City for the 1946 NAAU tournament. From left: Scott, Ben Conner, Dick Hauser, Leo Thomsen, Curt Stein, Lowell Lange, Harry Horn.

opponents to win the title. Jimmy Miller (Ithaca YMCA), won the 145-pound class, and Curt Stein placed third. At 155, Harry Horn almost won the tournament, losing in the finals to Bob Roemer 3–2.

Scott could not have been more pleased with the outcome. Conner had placed third, and the high schoolers were outstanding— Hauser and Lange won, Horn took second, and Stein third. Participation in these National AAU tournaments was to be one of the hallmarks of Scott's college coaching career. Besides the experience they provided his wrestlers, they also served to give tiny Cornell College a much higher profile in the wrestling community. This was the last time Scott took less than a full team to the tournament.

The real action for Scott, however, took place behind the scenes. Scott said, "I saw a Newton sweatshirt go by and I grabbed the kid and said, 'Say, whatever happened to Rodger Snook?' And he said, 'Well, Rodger just got out of the service. He's over there getting ready to weigh in. He's not in shape, he hasn't wrestled or anything during the war and he's just going to come out more for the fun of it.' So I went over to Snook and he remembered me and said, 'Coach, you won't want anything to do with me after you see me wrestle. I haven't been on the mat at all. I'll be terrible.' And he was! Some guy beat him right away. But I knew what he could do. So I said, 'Listen Snook, I want you at Cornell and you'll enjoy it.' I remembered that he liked the idea of a small college. His application beat me home. None of the other coaches had paid any attention to Snook because he had done so poorly." Scott often said that Rodger Snook was his greatest recruiting coup.

Scott also had a discussion with Al Partin. Al was in the New York area, just out of the service after four years in the Navy. He was wrestling for the West Side YMCA and working out with Henry Wittenberg. Al had entered the competition in the 175-pound weight class, where he lost to Harry Lanzi (Newton, New Jersey).

Al had been state champion his senior year at Proviso High School in Maywood, Illinois, the same high school where Cornell's Coach Barker had recruited both Frank Preston and Fred Bishop. In fact, Partin, Preston, Bishop, and Chuck Bryant were all teammates there at one point in time. Bryant, who wrestled at Purdue, later became the Cornell College wrestling coach from 1952 to 1959.

Claude Reeck, the coach at Purdue, who had been a teammate of Scott's at Cornell College, had contacted Partin and wanted him to come to Purdue. He insisted that Partin come for an interview, even though Al would be on the GI Bill. When he heard this, Scott said, "Look Al, I have an application right here, just fill it out and send it in." It arrived the following week. Al Partin never visited Purdue.

Scott drove Conner and the high school boys back to Mount Vernon. The boys got along well with Scott, and they appreciated the fact that he was not overbearing and just let them wrestle.

It All Comes Together

A few days later Scott met again with the parents of Hauser, Thomsen, and Lange at the Hauser restaurant. He told the parents that he would like the boys to come to Cornell and that he had arranged for scholarships for the three of them. They would have to pay for their rooms and work for their board. (In 1947 tuition at Cornell was $457, rooms were $100, and board was $280.) He suggested that they think seriously about it and come down for a formal visit as soon as possible. They visited the campus soon thereafter, as Scott had suggested.

Hauser had more or less made up his mind to go to Cornell, and Thomsen had too. The clincher perhaps was a conversation the two had with McCuskey where he indicated that even if they won their challenge match, he would still favor his seniors. This did not sit well with either Hauser or Thomsen. They both decided to go to Cornell. Lowell was undecided; McCuskey wanted him at Iowa Teachers and even paid him and his parents a visit. In the end, knowing that Hauser and Thomsen were going to Cornell, Lowell decided to join them. As he put it, "I had reason to go to Iowa Teachers, but I wasn't sold, and on the trip to New York City I got to know Scott. He was a guy you couldn't help but like. He had an uncanny memory for names, and no one could tell a story better."

Thus began Scott's incredibly successful effort to assemble his team. This talented trio—Dick Hauser, Leo Thomsen, and Lowell Lange—were virtually joined at the hip for the next four years, thanks to the freshmen rule. Scott's securing the West Waterloo threesome turned out to be one of the greatest recruiting coups in the history of collegiate wrestling.

Later that spring, Fred Dexter, out of the service, enrolled at the University of Iowa but did not feel comfortable there. He withdrew after a few weeks and was on his way to Cedar Falls to meet with Dave McCuskey about possibly enrolling at Iowa Teachers. He thought he would stop by Mount Vernon on the way, to talk to Scott. When he told Scott what he was up to, Scott said, "Fred, there's no need for you to go all the way up there. Just fill in this application and I'll see what I can do to get you in." This was easier said than done.

Fred Dexter was from a troubled home, and his absentee record at Davenport High School was roughly equivalent to one full year of academic work. In spite of missing that much work, however, he had a B-/C+ average. He had been in the service from September 1943 until December 1945. Scott's argument to admissions was that Dexter had done remarkably well considering all the class time he had missed. Dexter was accepted and never had any serious academic problems, except for being ineligible for one semester of his sophomore year.

Then, in the late fall of 1946, Scott caught another break. Kent Lange, Lowell's older brother by two years and another West Waterloo

The trio recruited from West Waterloo High School, from left: Dick Hauser, Leo Thomsen, Lowell Lange.

wrestler, was just out of the service and was applying to college. He applied to both Iowa State and Cornell. When he was accepted at Iowa State, he called Cornell admissions and told them he needed a decision on his application as soon as possible. Scott got behind it, and the office called back a couple of hours later to say he was in. Kent Lange was to start classes on February 1, 1947, for the second semester, and would be eligible to wrestle immediately. Meanwhile, he moved down to Mount Vernon, stayed in one of the dormitories that had been occupied by the Navy personnel, and begin to get in shape by working out with the rest of the team.

The veterans Rodger Snook, Fred Dexter, Al Partin, and Kent

Lange all took advantage of the GI Bill.

Scott had now assembled the heart of his team, men who were to wrestle all four years and graduate together in 1950. Four were from West Waterloo High School.

Of course, the heady recruiting days were not without their disappointments. Scott was unsuccessful in getting Bill Nelson, a high school champion from Eagle Grove, into Cornell. Nelson went on to win three NCAA championships for Iowa Teachers College, as well as three NAAU titles, and made the 1948 Olympic team.

Another loss was Harry Horn, who finally made it to Cornell in 1948 but was never really eligible academically, although he could wrestle in AAU events and the Olympic trials. Scott said he loaned Harry twenty dollars after the Olympic trials and never saw him again.

Recruiting Wizardry

In retrospect, what Paul Scott achieved in one year was nothing short of miraculous. He began 1946 with no team; he took two wrestlers to the YMCA tournament in Waterloo and one man to the NAAU tournament in New York City. But he was determined to build a competitive team for the next year. During the 1946 season he drove more than 5,000 miles for wrestling-related activities, using two vehicles, one provided by the college. Incredibly, within weeks of the final national tournament, Scott had assembled one of the strongest teams in the history of the sport. In terms of exposure and recruiting, it was also the most productive year in the history of the Cornell College.

As we have seen, Scott reaped the harvest of several years of cultivating future wrestlers, refereeing matches and spotting talent, making an indelible impression on young men, and inspiring trust and confidence in a brief meeting. He was a great salesman as well, and he had his sales pitch down pat. Cornell offered a good education and a beautiful campus. Somehow he was able to work around its athletic facilities, which did not compare favorably with those at larger schools (and Iowa Teachers' West Gym in particular). Scott, however, had hit upon the lure of traveling to national tournaments to tantalize those landlocked midwestern wrestlers.

As he recounted later, "Well, if you come to Cornell, you're going to wrestle on both coasts, because I'd known that the NAAU meets would be in one part of the country and the NCAA in the other and then another trip to New Orleans for the Sugar Bowl the following year.

"That was attractive bait to get these kids. Because to stay at Iowa, about the farthest trip they would get would be to Wisconsin and Minnesota, and if they sent anyone to a national meet, he had to be a Big Ten champion, and I took all my kids. That helped me recruit kids, and it helped them become better wrestlers because they got a lot of experience that a lot of the other kids were denied because they didn't get to go to these meets."

Scott recognized talent and excellent technique, and the fact that the heart of his team came from West Waterloo High School was not just a happy accident. He was well aware of the superior coaching those young men had already received.

The West Waterloo Connection

Much of the success of the Cornell College team of 1947 can be traced to the wrestling program at West Waterloo (Iowa) High School. In those days, Waterloo was a city of about 50,000 population, with the Cedar River flowing through its middle. It was a blue-collar town with the principal support coming from the packing and farm machinery industries represented by Rath Packing and the John Deere Tractor Works. Also in the Cedar Valley, eight miles to the west, was the much smaller town of Cedar Falls, home of Iowa State Teachers College.

A series of legendary coaches put their stamp on West Waterloo High wrestling. The first was Finn Eriksen. A native of Denmark, Eriksen immigrated to the U.S. in 1922 at the age of 17 after graduating from high school. He spoke little English and worked on a farm with a Danish family in Kimballton, Iowa, near Court Bluffs. In 1925 he attended Grand View College in Des Moines, where he took courses to prepare himself to pass the test to become a U.S. citizen. He also competed in gymnastics, at which he had excelled in Denmark.

The following year he wound up at Iowa Teachers, where he struggled for a time to master the language and subject matter. He was also exposed to the sport of wrestling, which had been introduced at the school only four years earlier. His first wrestling coach, Paul Bender, was replaced in 1931 by Dave McCuskey, who coached Eriksen in his senior year and remained the Teachers coach for 22 years, before leaving for the University of Iowa after the 1952 season.

Eriksen continued his education at Columbia University, receiving his master's degree in physical education in 1932. While in New York he worked out at the New York Athletic Club and represented the club in competition. He also added new techniques to his arsenal.

Eriksen's first high school coaching job was at New Hampton (Iowa) High School, where he developed a successful wrestling program. He then moved to West Waterloo in 1935 and began to build the most successful program in the state. He also introduced an innovative junior high program for younger wrestlers. It was in this outreach program that he first encountered Dick Hauser (at Sloan Wallace Junior High) and Leo Thomsen and Lowell Lange (at West Junior High).

Bob Appleby, a schoolmate of Hauser's, remembered those days when they were first introduced to wrestling: "Finn Eriksen came to Sloan Wallace on Mondays, Wednesdays and Fridays as P.E. instructor. On these days we, all boys, would line up in the small gym in clean white t-shirts and shorts. (They had to be clean and white to pass Finn's inspection.) We would do calisthenics and then we all, Finn included, would run around the block on which the school was situated."

"Finn was a disciplinarian. He always brought a paddle, about two feet long, to class. He would use it only if one of us talked out of turn. On those days Finn would encourage us to stay after school to learn a little about wrestling. Naturally, Dick Hauser and I participated, and Finn would put a couple of blankets on the floor of this small gym and he would work with us on fundamentals of wrestling: Referee's Position, Winglock, Switch, and some take-downs."

It was not until 1942 that Eriksen's team finally won the coveted state high school championship, held for the first time in Waterloo. The Wahawks won again the following year.

In April 1943 Eriksen received a commission in the Navy to be an athletic director for fledgling pilots, making sure that they were physically fit and drilling them in swimming, hand-to-hand combat, and wrestling. Eriksen said, "When I left, we had just reached the peak at West Waterloo. I had started Hauser wrestling in the seventh grade and had coached Lange for two years. I can remember when I first arrived at West that we would distribute student tickets on Mondays for wrestling, but no one came. The crowds started picking up, though, when we started winning."

When he returned to Waterloo in 1946, he was appointed director of health and physical Education for the entire Waterloo Public School System: 32 schools from kindergarten through high school. After his appointment he gradually introduced wrestling instruction to every junior high in the district.

He kept his hand in wrestling primarily though officiating at all levels, including 28 state high school tournaments and many collegiate conference tournaments, as well as NCAA championships. In 1952 he was one of the first Americans to serve as wrestling official and mat judge for the Olympic Games in Helsinki, Finland—where he witnessed Iowa wrestler Bill Smith win the gold medal. Eriksen conducted clinics for coaches, officials, and wrestlers and authored many articles in national publications. He served for many years as the high school representative to wrestling's national rules committee.

Eriksen retired in 1975 after 37 years of service to the citizens of Waterloo. He was inducted into the National Wrestling Hall of Fame in 1982. He died in 1992.

When Coach Eriksen left to go into the service, Roy Jarrard was selected to take his place as coach at West Waterloo High. He was perhaps the most underrated coach in Iowa high school wrestling lore, holding the unenviable position between two Hall of Fame coaches, Eriksen and Bob Siddens.

Jarrard was a 1930 graduate of the University of Iowa, where he wrestled for Mike Howard. He coached at Cherokee High School for several years, taking the team to the state championship 1939. West Waterloo was a difficult transition for Jarrard. Some of the boys on the team he inherited had been coached by Eriksen since junior high school, and all the juniors and seniors on the team had won the last two state championships.

Jarrard's coaching style was different from Eriksen's, and all he would hear from the boys after he demonstrated a move was, "Ho, that's not the way Coach Eriksen taught us." He finally had to take the veterans aside and explain to them that they did not have to do it his way, but there were all those young people he had to teach. They cooperated and went on to win another championship. They would win two more with Hauser, Thomsen, and Lange all winning in their senior year, 1946. Dick Hauser said that Jarrard was never given enough credit for his contribution to West Waterloo wrestling.

Jarrard coached West Waterloo through the 1949/50 season,

when Bob Siddens took over. When Jarrard left, he decided to go back to farming in Waverly, Iowa. He also taught physics at Waverly–Shell Rock High School until 1971. He died in 1994 at the age of 88.

Finn Eriksen had played a major role in getting Siddens the head coaching job at West Waterloo, and his recommendation turned out to be an excellent one. Siddens had been a solid wrestler at Eagle Grove High School before competing at Iowa Teachers. He was a varsity starter but had the misfortune of wrestling in the same weight classes as two of the great Teachers stars, Bill Nelson and Bill Smith. Upon graduation, he coached one year at Eagle Grove.

Siddens won state titles in his first two years at West Waterloo, where he was to coach for 27 years, amassing a record 327 dual meet wins—with one streak of 88 straight—and only 26 losses. His Wahawks team won 11 state team titles and had 14 undefeated seasons.

His wrestlers went on to win 19 Big Six titles, nine NCAA championships, and an Olympic gold medal. Best known as "Dan Gable's coach," Siddens also coached Dale Anderson, who won two NCAA titles for Michigan State. Gable won two for Iowa State and also won a world championship in 1971 and an Olympic gold medal in Munich in 1972.

Siddens was one of the most respected of all college referees, officiating in 27 NCAA championships. He traveled all over the country for many years, conducting clinics for wrestlers and officials. He made a major contribution to the sport and was inducted into the National Wrestling Hall of Fame in 1980. He is retired and resides in Waterloo with his wife Joyce. They have six children.

According to historian Jay Hammond, only three high schools have achieved double digits in individual NCAA titles. Tulsa Central leads with 25 titles, West Waterloo is next with 12, and Granby High School in Norfolk, Virginia, has 10.

Coaching the Team

Coaches will tell you that team chemistry is hard to predict. On the face of it, one would not have predicted that a blend of true freshmen and war veterans, most of whom were also freshmen, would make for a unified whole. Their ages ranged from the Waterloo High trio, who were 18, to Al Partin, who was 24. However, the team coalesced in this instance because of several factors: Scott was a great mentor for the younger men. The veterans were glad to be at Cornell under the GI Bill, and they were focused—on wrestling and on obtaining their degrees in four years' time. All but one of the team were members of the same fraternity, Delta Phi Rho, commonly known at the Delts. And everyone recognized how talented the young Waterloo trio were. Lowell Lange said that the thought of losing never crossed their minds (recalling Paul Newman's line in *The Hustler*: "When you're good and you know you're good, it's the greatest feeling in the world"). Such a positive, confident mind set was an irresistible influence on the rest of the team.

Great coaches tweak their systems to fit their athletes, rather than fit the athlete to the system, and that was Scott's philosophy: let each man develop his own style, rather than superimpose a certain style. "Well, I thought that a lot of coaches made the mistake of trying to make everyone do it the same way, and they didn't take in the matter of individual differences in the structure of the fella's body as much of a set up and all," said Scott. "And they'd try to mold the guy, all the same way, and I never did that. I'd just find the strongest points the kid had and emphasized that with him, and it paid off because they were able to kind of be their own coaches, rather than being stereotyped into being certain ways."

Coach Scott was not known to be a technician in the manner of his competitor coaches Dave McCuskey and Art Griffith, who were keen students of the advances in technique. This is not to say his boys were not well trained. Scott ran a hard two-hour practice. This included a 15-20 minute session with his top men, grouped by weight class, starting on their feet against opponents who would rotate in one-minute intervals. Lowell Lange said it was the hardest drill he ever experienced, a sentiment shared by Al Partin.

Scott admitted that he never really laid down any training rules. "I know Hauser and Thomsen both smoked," said Scott, "but it didn't bother me as long as they won." When Scott was asked by Hauser's dad when he recruited him, "What are you going to do about Dick's smoking?" he replied, "As long as he can beat everybody in America, why would I complain about his smoking?" (It should be noted that this was an era when cigarette advertising was all-pervasive, and smoking was endorsed by celebrities, entertainers, and athletes alike. Indeed, the back cover of the 1948 U.S. Olympic Team Trials program featured baseball stars Ted Williams, Joe DiMaggio, and Stan Musial in an ad for Chesterfields.)

Scott counted on his considerable motivational skills to bring out the most of each man. "I relate well to athletes, I could motivate them, instill confidence in them, and get them to put out everything they had." Moreover, his wrestlers came to know that he felt genuine affection for them. "Oh yes, I loved all of them," he said years later. "Yes, they were a wonderful bunch of guys. Yes, there are lots of stories to tell about those guys."

The Magical Season

1947 Pre-Season

The 1946/47 school year saw the total Cornell enrollment climb to 824 students, 415 of whom were men. (Today the student body numbers 1,200 students.) The new Class of 1950 was the largest on campus, with a total enrollment of 261 students—139 men and 122 women; 48 of the freshmen men had served in the military.

In addition to his duties as athletic director, Scott began the fall schedule by coaching the cross-country team, a job he loved. The team finished its 1946 season as Midwest Conference champions.

Wrestling practice began right after the cross-country and football seasons ended. Scott was somewhat surprised to find that, in contrast to the previous year, he now had 46 eager participants, including two men from his cross-country team. No one was turned away, in spite of the fact that workout space was limited. Alumni Gymnasium was completed in 1908, well before wrestling rooms could have been anticipated. To accommodate the bumper crop of wrestlers, Scott took over the women's exercise room on the second floor of the gym—not exactly something that would be tolerated today!

Although the turnout was impressive, more than two thirds of the men had never been on a wrestling mat before. Of the wrestlers with some experience, there was a mix of true freshman and veterans; some had four years of eligibility, and others, from teams as far back as 1942 and 1943, needed only one or more years to graduate. Only a few men had wrestled for Scott in the previous season.

The time-honored process for determining which wrestler would start at a particular weight class was the "wrestle-off" or challenge match, which was considered sacrosanct. Usually there was a "ladder" posted in the wrestling room, listing each man by weight class. Sometimes there were small, round tags placed on hooks. At the end of each season the departing seniors' tags would be removed and all remaining would move up a notch on the ladder, assuming they all remained in the same weight class. But with no previous season to fall back on, Scott was starting from scratch—there were no tags to move up.

Scrimmages began in earnest the first week, followed by several wrestle-offs in preparation for the first meet, with the Fort Dodge YMCA. Things quickly sorted themselves out. It became readily apparent that the trio from West Waterloo was clearly a cut above the rest, as were Rodger Snook, Fred Dexter, Al Partin, and Kent Lange (who would be eligible at the start of the second semester).

Scott's challenge was not to separate the men from the boys, but rather to meld the men and the boys into a cohesive unit. In order to do this, he had to figure out a way to integrate his new starters with the veterans returning from his successful 1943 team, particularly the two men from Mount Vernon, Arlo Ellison and Pic Littell.

Littell was easy, since he would start at 155 pounds until Kent Lange became eligible. The main problem for Scott was how to utilize Arlo Ellison, one of the stars of his 1943 team, into the lineup. Ellison could not beat either Lowell Lange or Rodger Snook in wrestle-offs. This was difficult for Ellison, and to his credit he contributed very effectively as a utility man, wrestling anywhere from 136 to 165 pounds, which gave Scott valuable flexibility in his lineup.

Scott always tried to insert as many men into the starting lineup as he could. Eventually, 17 men started in at least one meet, and 22 were entered in open tournaments. He would also arrange with the opposing coaches to wrestle one or two exhibition matches prior to the start of dual meets, for those wrestlers who could not break into the starting lineup.

Remarkably, in the eight-man starting lineup, seven men— Hauser, Thomsen, Lowell Lange, Rodger Snook, Fred Dexter, and Al Partin, plus Kent Lange—remained as starters not only for the first season but for their entire four year careers at Cornell College. We call them the "Magnificent Seven."

The Starting Lineup

This, then, was the makeup of the team at the beginning of the 1947/48 season:

Dick Hauser would wrestle 121 pounds and 128 pounds. The most explosive and entertaining wrestler on the team, he was every coach's dream as the lead-off man.

Leo Thomsen would wrestle 128 pounds and 136 pounds. He was the most conventional of the West Waterloo wrestlers, with a well-balanced attack and defense.

Lowell Lange would wrestle 136 pounds and 145 pounds. One of the greatest "control" wrestlers in history, he was the most reliable man on the team, although not known for his pinning ability. Gerry Leeman said of him, "He was tenacious and deliberate; he made no mistakes."

This West Waterloo trio, continuing together from high school to college, had the advantage of shared training and experiences. However, they also faced disadvantages: they were only 18 and would for the most part be wrestling against veterans who were two to four years older and

51

more mature; and they would be wrestling at the same weight classes they wrestled in high school, in spite of the fact that they were still "growing boys." Making weight was to become increasingly difficult.

Rodger Snook was next at 145 pounds and 155 pounds. Though not as strong on his feet as the West Waterloo trio, he was the most aggressive pinner on the team, with one of the best cradles ever seen.

Kent Lange would wrestle 145 pounds and 155 pounds. Both he and Snook met some of the toughest competitors in the history of the sport, wrestling their entire careers in the shadow of Teachers stars Bill Koll followed by Keith Young, both three-time national champions at 145.

Fred Dexter and **Al Partin,** who both weighed about 185 pounds, would wrestle anywhere from 165 pounds to 175 pounds and heavyweight. Partin actually preferred to wrestle heavyweight. They, too, would face two of the greatest wrestlers of any era in Bill Nelson and Bill Smith from Teachers.

All of these Cornell College men were to win either an NCAA or NAAU title or finish no lower than third in one of those tournaments.

Scott had three lightweights to fill in at 121 pounds whenever the Waterloo trio moved up a class: **John Gregg, Ben McAdams,** and **Dale Sherrill**. All were to wrestle at least one dual meet.

At the middle weights, he would have **Arlo Ellison** and **Pic Littell,** the two veterans from Mount Vernon, and at the heavier weights, **Joe Pelisek, Charles Voyce**, and **Ben Conner.** All but Voyce and Pelisek were to win the Midwest Conference championship at least one time.

There were to be other wrestlers added to the mix in the years to come.

The Ninth Man – Rick Meredith

"I carried a typewriter in one hand and the bag of tape in the other," Gordon "Rick" Meredith '47 wrote. "I got rich sending stories to papers in Cedar

Rapids, Des Moines, Waterloo, and Chicago. Some months I made over $100 (at 10 cents an inch) to supplement my GI Bill check of $109."

Rick Meredith entered Cornell in 1941 and attended for two years. He went out for football and wrestling and managed to make the wrestling squad. He was active in student affairs and with sports journalism in particular.

In 1943 he went into the Marine V-12 program at Oberlin College, then in 1944 became a naval officer in the U.S. Naval Reserve program at Northwestern. He began serving as deck officer on LSTs in the Pacific and was commanding officer of USS LST 696. His 22 months in the Pacific included invasions of Leyte Gulf and Okinawa.

After his release he drove back from Californian in his 1930 Oldsmobile to complete his last year at Cornell. In a conversation with Scott about becoming manager of the team, he sensed that Scott did not think much of the car he was driving. He bought a 1938 Plymouth that had hardly ever been driven, and this sealed the deal. The Plymouth would be part of the "armada" that transported the team on its signature road trips, and Meredith would be team manager.

Rick Meredith was the unsung hero of the 1947 team. Bearing in mind that Scott was also the athletic director, Meredith, as manager, assisted with travel arrangements, provided his vehicle for transportation, served as trainer when the team was away from home, typed papers for the team, was sports editor of the student paper, and submitted results of all the meets, with narrative, to the Des Moines *Register*, Cedar Rapids *Gazette*, Chicago *Tribune*, and of course the local paper, the Mount Vernon–Lisbon *Sun*. Scott described him as "a living encyclopedia of sports and a darned good newspaper man."

Meredith's columns in both the student paper and the local press, along with Scott's popularity with everyone including the townspeople of Mount Vernon, who embraced the team, contributed to a groundswell of support for the wrestling team. Even folks who were not particularly familiar with the sport caught the wrestling fever that swept the campus and the town.

The Magical Season

From the first meet on, the team enjoyed the support of the students as well as the town, which then numbered 1,441. According to Scott, "Students would start camping out in front of the gym at noon and build fires on the sidewalk to keep warm. The gym seated about 1,000 but it would be packed all the way to the very top. They hung from the rafters, literally." This enthusiasm continued all the way through the team's four years at Cornell.

The school's colors were purple and white, and its teams were referred to as "the Purple." The wrestlers took the floor resplendent in purple boxing robes, and they wore white shorts over purple tights. They competed stripped to the waist, which was permitted until the 1960s.

Scott scheduled 12 dual meets, the toughest schedule in the school's history. Cornell would encounter the Big Six champion (Iowa State), the Big Ten champion (University of Illinois), an eastern swing that would include the EIWA champion (Lehigh), and the two leading independent schools, Iowa Teachers and Michigan State.

The first two meets of the season were essentially warm-up matches. The first was at home on December 15, 1946, against the Fort Dodge YMCA, a team composed primarily of returning servicemen and high-schoolers. Scott had everyone down to his lowest weight class. The most interesting match was between Al Partin and Bob Siddens, former Eagle Grove wrestler, which Siddens won 8–7. Cornell won the meet 26–8.

Next was the Ottumwa Naval Pre-Flight School. Everyone wrestled up one weight class, and Scott inserted his cross-country star, Ben McAdams, at 121 pounds, who did not disappoint. Cornell won 33–3.

After Christmas break, the first big dual meet of the new year was in Ames with Iowa State on January 11. The Big Six champion was wrestling under its new coach, Ray Stone, successor to the legendary Hugo Otopalik. Cornell had won their last encounter back in 1943.

Main Street, downtown Mount Vernon, in 1947

A large crowd of 3,000 sat in awe as the Cornellians racked up six straight wins, four falls, and two decisions. Hauser led off with a pin, followed by Thomsen's defeat of Charles Nelson, also a former state champion. Scott moved Ellison into the 136-pound class, where he won, and Lowell Lange, wrestling at 145 pounds, pinned his man.

What most shocked the home crowd was Rodger Snook's sensational pin of Richard Ditsworth in the 155-pound class. Ditsworth had placed third in the NCAA meet the year before. Fred Dexter then pinned his man. Al Partin lost a decision.

Glenn Brand, a future NCAA and Olympic champion, pinned senior Charles Voyce at heavyweight. After his freshman year at Cornell, Voyce had attended Annapolis for a year, returned to Cornell for another year, and then joined the Air Corps. After four years in the service and now married, he was back at Cornell. The final score was 26–8, a decisive team victory that certainly got the attention of the Iowa wrestling community.

The following week the team went to Peoria, Illinois, to crush Bradley University 34–0.

The Epic Dual

Most collegiate wrestling fans believe that the first great rivalry in Iowa collegiate wrestling was Iowa vs. Iowa State. Not so! In the postwar

55

period, the first great contests were between little Cornell College of Mount Vernon and Iowa Teachers College of Cedar Falls. The last time the two schools had met, in 1942, Cornell defeated Teachers 19–11; the 1943 meet had been cancelled because of the war.

In 1947 the two schools were to do battle on Friday, January 24,

Coach Scott talks strategy with (from left) Leo Thomsen, Lowell Lange, and Dick Hauser, before dual meet with Iowa State Teachers College, January 24, 1947.

at 8 P.M. in what was billed as the mythical wrestling championship of Iowa. Against one common opponent, Iowa State, both had scored lopsided victories. (The Teachers–Iowa State meet had taken place only three days earlier, and Paul Scott had attended, scouting the Teachers team.)

Mount Vernon fans following the team to Cedar Falls were urged to go early, since a sell-out crowd was expected. People from Waterloo had ordered a huge block of tickets because so many former West Waterloo stars were scheduled to appear. (In the first four weight classes, six of the eight wrestlers were from West Waterloo High School.) It was estimated that 3,700 fans attended, although the posted capacity of the Teachers College field house was only 2,200. The meet lived up to the hype.

Coaches Paul Scott and Dave McCuskey both made last-minute lineup changes. The much-anticipated duel between Bill Koll and Rodger Snook would have to wait, since Teachers' 155-pound starter, Dick Black, was out of the lineup due to an injury, meaning that Koll would move up to face Pic Littell. Snook would meet Neal Johnson, another West Waterloo veteran, at 145 pounds. Dr. Hugh Linn was the referee.

The feature match of the evening was expected to be the lead-off match at 121 pounds between two former West Waterloo stars — Jim Stoyanoff, a veteran of Teachers, and Dick Hauser of Cornell — both three-time state champions. Stoyanoff had won state titles in 1940, '41, and '42, and he had never lost a bout to a man in his own weight class. Hauser held state titles for 1944, '45, and '46.

Scott said that the first period, which began from the standing position, was "the best three minutes of wrestling on the feet that I'd ever seen." Neither man scored a takedown. Hauser rode Stoyanoff the entire second period. In the third period, Hauser quickly reversed and rode Stoyanoff for the rest of the match. Stoyanoff looked tired at the end. Hauser won the match 4–0, including two minutes of riding time.

At 128 pounds, Teachers' Gerry Leeman, NCAA champion, defeated freshman Leo Thomsen 10–2, taking him down three times. Leeman modestly said he thought the difference was simply a matter

Dick Hauser (top) in his match with Jim Stoyanoff of Iowa Teachers in the dual meet held on January 24, 1947 at Iowa Teachers College. Hauser won the match by decision 4-0.

of experience. Both men were to make the Olympic team in 1948.

At 136 pounds, Lowell Lange defeated Russ Bush 3–0. There was no takedown, but Lange rode Bush out in the second period and escaped to his feet in the third. Both men were from West Waterloo, and both were to win an NCAA title that year, Lange at 136 pounds and Bush at 128 pounds.

Rodger Snook then won decisively over Neal Johnson 6–0. The score was then 9–3 in favor of Cornell.

The critical match of the evening turned out to be between the defending NCAA champion Bill Koll and Pic Littell at 155 pounds.

At all the practice sessions during the week, Scott had been telling his middleweights that if they were to wrestle this guy Koll, "Whatever you do, don't try to stand up when you are on the bottom because he will hip lock you and throw you on your head." (That maneuver was called a "slam.") Sure enough, early in the match Littell attempted to escape by standing up and was knocked out. If he had been unable to finish the match, it would have been considered a pin, giving Teachers five points. However, they were able to revive poor Littell with smelling salts, and he survived the 9-minute ordeal. Littell lost 8–1, thereby giving up only 3 points. He would forever be a hero in the eyes of the Cornell fans.

Bill Koll, Iowa Teachers (hidden) in action against Iowa State, initiating one of his famous hip throws.

It is said that the "slam rule" was put into effect because of Bill Koll. In 1951 all slams were ruled illegal: "A contestant who lifts his opponent off the mat is responsible for his safe return to the mat."

At 165 pounds, Bill Nelson defeated Al Partin 7–2. Al once said that if he had wrestled him 100 times he could not have beaten him. At 175 pounds, Leroy Alitz defeated Charles Voyce 10–4. The score was now 12–9 in favor of Teachers. In the final match, Cornell's Fred Dexter went all out to try to pin Jim Jensen but settled for a 4-0 win. The final score: 12–12.

In retrospect, this was one of the greatest dual meets in wrestling history, with so many outstanding coaches and athletes participating: two Hall of Fame coaches (Scott and McCuskey), six Hall of Fame wrestlers, four Olympians, seven NCAA or NAAU champions, nine high school champions, six boys from West Waterloo alone, and notably, 12 war veterans out of the 16 wrestlers. Scott said, "I'll never forget this meet as long as I live." What has made it a classic was the fact that it ended in a tie.

The truth is, if either team had won it, only those who were there would remember it today.

In his book From *Gotch to Gable*, wrestling historian Mike Chapman relates Scott's reminiscing many years later about the Teachers rivalry: "We were the most bitter rivals, but we had great respect for each other. For the most part we wrestled on pretty equal terms. But that meet with Teachers in 1947...I would have to say that's as fine a wrestling meet as I have ever seen."

The following morning Scott went down to the gym. He had anticipated that he might encounter Clair Littell—renowned Cornell professor of history and political science, and father of Pic—who would "chew him out" for having put his son in harm's way. So Scott took the initiative when he saw him and said, "I want to shake the hand of the father of one of the gutsiest guys that ever wrestled the sport." Scott remembered that "this kind of took him off balance," because he then backed off.

University of Illinois

The last meet of the semester was at home on January 31, 1947, against the Big Ten champion, Illinois. Scott was eager to reverse the beating Illinois had given Cornell in 1942. This was to be a battle of the Cornell lightweight stars against the outstanding Illinois heavier-weight contingent, including NCAA champion Dave Shapiro wrestling at 165 pounds. Another standing-room-only crowd of more than 1,000 awaited the wrestlers.

Both coaches made adjustments in their lineups. Illinois coach Harold E. "Hek" Kenney elected to wrestle Lou Kachiroubas up at 136 pounds to face Lowell Lange; Lou had been runner-up to Gerry Leeman in the 128-pound weight class in the 1946 NCAA championship. Scott moved Arlo Ellison up to 155 pounds, giving away 19 pounds to his opponent.

Hauser led off with a sensational pin of Dean Ryan in 5:02, followed by Leo Thomsen's pin of Bill Mann in 7:19. Lowell Lange then completely shut down Kachiroubas 7–1.

The pivotal matches turned out to be in the middle-weight classes. Rodger Snook took a tough 9–6 decision from Joe Garcia, and Arlo Ellison, in the match of the meet, scored a stunning 16–14 overtime thriller against Stan Lee, after trailing 6–1 at one point and being tied 10–10 after regulation.

Dave Shapiro soundly defeated Al Partin 17–7, and Norman Anthonisen pinned Joe Pelisek in 4:09. A mild upset took place at heavyweight, where Chuck Gottfried decisioned a previously undefeated Fred Dexter 6–2.

Cornell won the meet 19–11.

Better Late Than Never

The Cornell team was eager to set off on its much-anticipated eastern swing. Before departure day, however, Scott was to add one more man to Cornell's contingent. How Dale Thomas came to rejoin the Cornell team is a story unto itself.

After the end of the 1943 school year, Thomas, then a Cornell junior, joined the Marine Corps and spent the next three years in the service, much of the time on various college campuses. Incredibly, he played guard in football at both Oberlin College and Ohio Wesleyan during the same football season. He taught school at Delma (Iowa) High School 1945–46, while also coaching boys' and girls' basketball, baseball, and softball.

After the war, Thomas enrolled at Purdue in the fall of 1946 to play football and wrestle. Thomas had been following the success of Cornell, and in December he quizzed Rick Meredith, his former teammate and now manager of the team. Did Scott harbor any animosity toward him because he had stayed at Purdue? The answer was No, without reservation. Would he be welcomed back at Cornell? Yes, of course. However, Meredith added, Scott did not see any reason for his coming back for the last semester of his senior year because he would not be eligible to wrestle.

Because Thomas lived in nearby Marion, he paid a visit to Scott during Christmas break. Scott told him that for eligibility he would need to get permission first from the Midwest Conference and then from the Big Ten commissioner. Thomas dutifully went to Coe College to see Dr. C. Ward Macy, acting commissioner of the Midwest Conference, and received clearance from him the next day.

Scott and Thomas then took the train to Chicago to plead their case to Kenneth "Tug" Wilson, the Big Ten commissioner, whose headquarters was in the old Sherman Hotel. (Wilson was the same individual who had ruled in the "Martin incident" the year before.) Arlo Ellison, Thomas's teammate from the 1943 team and now returned from the service, went along.

Essentially Thomas, who was a bit of an opportunist, told Wilson that he had been kind of duped into going to Purdue and wanted to transfer back to Cornell, where he had spent his first three years. Wilson, who had been athletic director at Northwestern and had no love for Purdue, said he saw no reason why not, and declared Thomas eligible for the second semester. Scott later recalled Wilson's explanation: "Why of course Thomas was eligible. He is a national champion there and should be permitted to finish school there and, after all, with the military service shuffling of students, there is nothing uncommon about athletes jumping from one school to another mid-year."

Needless to say, the Purdue coach, Claude Reeck (a teammate of Scott's at Cornell College) was not amused when he found out about Thomas's defection. According to historian Jay Hammond, this would go down as one of the most bizarre transfers of all time.

Scott had now used all the tools at his disposal—the GI Bill, the freshman rule, and now a liberal transfer policy—to assemble the team.

Road Trips

Thank goodness Paul Scott loved to drive, because he logged a staggering number of miles transporting this team during its four years at Cornell. With the end of the war, gasoline rationing had been lifted, as had the 35 m.p.h. speed limit; gasoline was still 15 cents per gallon. When Scott had enticed his recruits with the promise of competitions in far-flung, exciting locales, he neglected to mention how they would get to those national meets and where they would stay. The mode of travel, as gleefully described by Scott, gives new meaning to the term "roughing it":

I had an old (1943) International station wagon that had plate glass windows in it and the doors that had been used as a grocery delivery truck [during the Navy training period]. It had two seats in the back that had places in the floor where you could clamp the seat hooks in there. So, I could take about eight guys and a lot of baggage, and then [Rick] Meredith, my team manager, had an old car of some kind, and he would drive that and one or two of the other guys. So I'd take about ten wrestlers, and Meredith and all the equipment, and we'd load up. I guess the old International Station wagon served us all the four years I coached here.

The center of gravity of that thing was about at windshield level and we'd just rock down. It's a wonder we weren't killed. A hard car to navigate with and cold. We didn't have a heater and we'd bundle up. Put blankets around the legs of the fellas and it was uncomfortable. Snow would drift in. Kids would put up with a lot of inconveniences because we didn't have a lot of money to travel with. I fed them mostly. Well, they didn't get to eat very much anyway because they were keeping their weight down.

Lodging was on a par with the condition of the automobiles and could best be described as "cheap." Again, in Scott's words:

> I'd go into a hotel and they had sample rooms where merchants could display their stuff, and I could get them to put cots in for $1.00 or $1.50 each. A lot of times I'd just work out a deal with the motel or hotel. We'd go to a motel and the guy would have it closed down for the winter and he'd say, "Well, I don't have any heat," and I'd say, "Well, I'll give you $1.00 apiece and put the guys up and we don't mind about that," and I'd have the guys put on all their sweat clothes. The other coaches around here thought that I had a lot of travel budget money, but I didn't. I took all my guys, and that gave the impression that we had lots of money, but we actually went on just a beggar's budget.

Ben McAdams remembers one incident that occurred on the eastern swing and was probably pretty typical of travels with the team. Ben was rooming with Al Partin, the senior member of the team, who for some unknown reason had brought only one pair of socks, which he dutifully washed out every night. One night, when they wound up staying in a motel that was above a service station, Al hung his socks to dry on a chair in front of the electric heater. What he didn't anticipate was that while they were asleep, the electricity for the heater was turned off. When Al awoke he found that his socks were solidly frozen. According to McAdams this was not a problem for Al, who simply beat the socks over the chair until the ice was gone and then promptly put them on.

There was plenty of excitement on these trips, and Scott had all he could do to control the rambunctious teenagers, all of whom wanted to sit in the front seats with their coach. Disputes were often settled by stopping the car to let the boys wrestle it out. Luckily no one got hurt.

Scott's road trips revealed one character flaw that did not escape the notice of his passengers: he was stubborn. Although he was sometimes directionally challenged, he refused to ask directions, with the result that on more than one occasion he ended up way off course. Stopping only at service stations when he needed gas, he would then casually ask some questions about his whereabouts or destination. The entourage eventually arrived at its destination, however, and safely.

The Eastern Swing

> The International was good for us as it had a back seat with a wood floor. The floor had a big hole in it, so we learned to stack three little wrestlers on top of each other and by the time we reached the next meet they were so sick of the fumes, they always made weight. And you recall we always won those weights 121–128 and 136. The other reason Coach Scott liked the International was that it would only go forward, which is what he always taught us, never move backwards on the mat.
>
> —RICK MEREDITH, *speaking at his induction into the*
> *Cornell College Hall of Fame, September 25, 1998*

The eastern road trip had actually been initiated by Coach Dick Barker in 1935 and had traditionally included Franklin and Marshall, where his mentor "Uncle" Charlie Mayser coached, and Army, home of his former wrestling star, the Olympian Lloyd Appleton. In addition, Barker would try to schedule the New York Athletic Club (NYAC). These trips were made in 1935, 1940, and 1941. Scott was to do him one better by scheduling four matches in all: Lehigh University, the strongest team in the East; Army; the McBurney YMCA in New York City; and the Ithaca YMCA in Ithaca, New York.

The "twin armada"—the intrepid International plus Meredith's

Plymouth—departed on Saturday, February 1, for the trip East. Included were all of the starting lineup plus backups (Ben McAdams, Pic Littell, Joe Pelisek, and Arlo Ellison), and lastly, Kent Lange, who had been waiting for his second-semester enrollment to begin and would be eligible by the time they arrived for the meet with Lehigh in Bethlehem, Pennsylvania, on Tuesday.

They headed east on the Lincoln Highway, which passed through the outskirts of Mount Vernon. This was America's first coast-to-coast highway, a 3,300-mile road stretching from New York to San Francisco, laid out in 1913 and completed in 1927. (The interstate highway system that we know today was the result of the Federal Highway Act of 1956, passed by the Eisenhower administration.) Cabin camps and motels were readily available along the way.

The first order of business was to pick up Dale Thomas. They met up with him in Logansport, Indiana, at the Anheuser Grill, owned by a Navy buddy of Meredith's, not far from the Purdue campus in West Lafayette. Thomas had wrestled for Purdue against Michigan earlier that evening. Thomas remembered, "They didn't even give me time to shower. They stuck me, all sweaty, in the back where there was a hole in the floorboard. By the time we got to Bethlehem, I had my death of cold and they made me go out and wrestle Lehigh."

Things did not get off to a good start in Bethlehem. They arrived on Tuesday afternoon and weighed in for the evening match. Scott had requested that two of his boys, Hauser and Thomsen, be allowed to wear headgear to protect their ears, which were pretty banged up. Unlike today, when headgear is mandatory, one had to request permission to wear it. Billy Sheridan, the legendary and sometimes crusty Lehigh coach, at first said okay, but later came back and said he had changed his mind, but that they could have the Lehigh trainer bandage their ears. Scott was furious and said, "No, thank you, we'll do it ourselves." Hauser and Thomsen were more than a little upset.

"We got there early in the evening," Meredith recalled, "and decided to look upstairs in their new gym to see if it looked like anybody would come on this snow-filled night, high on a hill. We poked our heads around the stairs and saw that every seat was filled. All the students had come early to get seats." Grace Hall, known as the Snake Pit, was packed with 2,500 avid wrestling fans who had braved the elements to see the match.

Scott had all of his men down to their competitive weights. Hauser led off with a pin against Pilgrim McRaven, a 28-year-old veteran from Tulsa who was to become an eastern champion in that season. This set the tone for the rest of the meet. Pins from Thomsen, Lowell Lange, and Rodger Snook followed. Snook pinned his opponent with his patented cradle, much to the delight of a contingent from Newton, who had come up to see him. Kent Lange in his first varsity match won by decision. Fred Dexter then pinned his man.

Dale Thomas, who was ill, struggled to get a decision. Hauser, who always sat next to Scott, said in a voice intentionally audible, "I thought you said this bum could wrestle."

In the most exciting bout of the evening, at heavyweight, Al Partin came from behind for another pin. The score was 36–0.

It was the most decisive defeat in the history of Lehigh wrestling, and the first time they had been shut out since 1914, by Navy.

Sports editor Fred Nonnemacher of the Bethlehem *Globe-Times* dubbed the Purple "the greatest college team I have ever seen in action in the 26 years I have been here." The rest of the trip was almost anti-climactic.

In a gesture that would be unheard of today, Scott allowed Al Partin to leave the team at this point to go to New York City to see his girlfriend. They would meet him back in Mount Vernon.

Next was Army, the following day. Ben McAdams took over at 121 pounds to allow the others to wrestle up one weight class. Rodger Snook pinned the Army star Stan Thevenet, from Bethlehem, Pennsylvania. Thevenet was last heard to say, as would many others, "I was beating him until he pinned me." Army was defeated 27–2.

Lloyd Appleton, the Army coach and a former star at Cornell College, said, "They're the top team ever to show in the east."

McBurney YMCA in New York City was next. Perhaps the best bouts of that meet were Kent Lange's defeat of NAAU champ Chris Soukas 7–6 at 165 pounds, and the 4–4 draw at 155 pounds between Rodger Snook and the veteran Joe Kissane. Snook came from behind with 10 seconds remaining to force a scoreless overtime. It would prove an important learning experience for Snook, since the two were to meet again.

When the boys got to Ithaca on Saturday, their last stop, they were pretty much out of steam. They faced the Ithaca YMCA, a team composed mainly of the best wrestlers from Cornell University and Ithaca College.

McAdams, Hauser, Thomsen, and Snook all pinned their men. The three Ithaca stars also won: Jimmy Miller defeated Kent Lange 8–3, Jim Larock pinned Littell, and Forbes Brown pinned Joe Pelisek. Cornell won the meet 23–13. The guys were happy to "get out of Dodge" and return to Mount Vernon.

By the end of this trip everyone was well aware of the strength of Cornell College wrestling.

Homestretch

The team had a week to recover from the arduous road trip and prepare for the University of Wisconsin at Madison on February 15.

Scott's plan once again was to move all his starters up one weight class, since he would have them cut weight for the big match with Michigan State the following weekend. He gave Dale Sherrill, another West Waterloo product, a shot at 121 pounds; he lost a close bout 3–2. Hauser won. Scott gave Leo Thomsen the night off and inserted Ellison at 136 pounds, who got a pin. Lowell Lange and Rodger Snook defeated their opponents. In the best match of the evening, at 165 pounds, Clarence Self, Wisconsin's best wrestler, defeated Al Partin 5–3. Dexter won at 175 pounds. At heavyweight, Dale Thomas was the victim of a fall in 5:50 to Bill Bennett. Leading 5–0, Thomas was caught with a roll, and Bennett used his 50-pound weight advantage to end the match abruptly. It was Thomas's first dual meet loss since 1942, 22 matches ago. Cornell won the meet 17–11.

Next on the schedule was Michigan State, coached by Fendley Collins, a protégé of Ed Gallagher's at Oklahoma State. For the first time in five matches, all of the Cornell regulars were down to their regular weight class.

The meet was at home, again with a packed house. Six of the visitors' eight men came from Oklahoma high schools, including four from Tulsa Central. Two of them, Joe Dickinson, 128 pounds, and Gale Mikles, 155 pounds, were National AAU champions in 1945.

Hauser pinned Gene MacDonald in 5:40. In a key match at 128 pounds, Dickinson (Michigan State) defeated Leo Thomsen 4–2. The two men were to meet again in the NCAA tournament.

Lowell Lange disposed of Michigan State's captain, "Iggy" Konrad, 4–0. Snook pinned his man. Gale Mikles defeated Kent Lange rather easily 7–0. Dexter won. Partin pinned his opponent, and at heavyweight, Thomas defeated the 220-pound Bob Maldegan 8–5.

Cornell crushed Michigan State 24–6. This was probably the most decisive win of the season, considering the caliber of the wrestling.

Next on the schedule was the Midwest Conference Championship on March 1. Because Cornell competed in all the other sports in the conference, Scott felt duty-bound to support wrestling, even though the Purple were head and shoulders above the rest of the teams participating. This year the four colleges that fielded teams for the conference championship were Cornell,

Carleton, Beloit, and the host school, Lawrence, in Appleton, Wisconsin.

Scott had everyone up a weight class, which meant that Johnny Gregg would wrestle at 121 pounds. Lowell Lange and Rodger Snook had the night off, replaced by Arlo Ellison and Kent Lange. Journeyman Bob Soper wrestled at 165 pounds and Ben Conner at 175. Senior Dale Thomas wrestled heavyweight. He had already won this tournament once, in 1942.

Cornell won all the weight classes except 165 pounds, where Bob Soper lost in the finals. This was Cornell's sixth straight conference championship.

On the night of March 3, at home, there was a full house for the Nebraska meet. Nebraska did not present a real threat to Cornell, and Scott again inserted Dale Sherrill at 121 pounds, where he once more disappointed Scott by earning only a draw. Arlo Ellison had an exciting match at 145 pounds, narrowly defeating his opponent 10–9.

Dale Thomas at heavyweight met Mike DiBiase, the star of the Nebraska team, who was 5'9", weighed 230 pounds, and had a 21" neck (he was also starting tackle on the football team). He had won 54 of his last 55 bouts and was the defending NAAU champion. Thomas was spotting DiBiase 45 pounds. The first period was cautious and scoreless. Each man broke out from the underneath position in the succeeding periods. They fought to a 1–1 tie, which was really a victory for Thomas. Cornell routed Nebraska 26–4.

The dual meet season ended with 12 wins, no losses, and one tie. The Purple had defeated the Big Six champions (Iowa State), the Big Ten champions (Illinois), and the EIWA champions (Lehigh), as well as one of the two leading independents (Michigan State), while drawing with the other (Iowa Teachers).

The last bit of business before the NCAA championship was the Iowa AAU Championship on March 7–8, the first resumption of that tournament since Iowa Teachers held it in 1942. It was especially important for Cornell and Teachers, since they did not have a true conference like the Big Ten or the EIWA. Cornell was to host this year in Mount Vernon. Scott was the chairman of Iowa State AAU wrestling and the man in charge of the meet. Scott loved these AAU tournaments because he could wrestle many men. In this instance he entered 22 of his squad.

Of the eleven weight classes, five corresponded to the Iowa high school brackets, and the top six paralleled NCAA Divisions. NCAA rules were used.

The team championship was between Cornell and Teachers. Unfortunately, three of Teachers' starters, Stoynoff, Leeman, and Koll, were injured and sat out the meet. The absence of these three men was a big disappointment to local fans, who had anticipated a replay of the 12–12 dual meet tie earlier in the season. Leeman and Koll, however, were on hand to offer mat-side advice. At one point Koll was heard to say, "I wonder why a school that puts out such top teams has such a little gym." He was of course referring to Cornell's Alumni Gymnasium.

In re-matches of the dual meet with Teachers, Lowell Lange once again defeated Russ Bush 4–1, and Rodger Snook defeated Neal Johnson 8–2. At 175, Dale Thomas easily defeated Leroy Alitz (Teachers) 7–3 (causing some to speculate that had Thomas been on the team during the first semester dual meet, Cornell might have won that meet). Cornell won the tournament handily.

The regular season was now over, and the team had two weeks to prepare for the NCAA championship. Scott had managed to "keep the team on the field"; they had no major health issues.

The NCAA Championship (March 28–29, 1947)

The most elusive goal in collegiate wrestling, the NCAA team championship, has been won by only 10 schools since the team title was officially recognized in 1934. Five schools have been multiple winners—

University of Oklahoma, Oklahoma A&M (now Oklahoma State), Iowa, Iowa State, and Minnesota—and five are one-time winners—Cornell College (1947), Iowa Teachers College, now University of Northern Iowa (1950), Penn State (1953), Michigan State (1967), and Arizona State (1988).

From 1934, six schools have been multiple winners — University of Oklahoma, Oklahoma A & M (now Oklahoma State), Iowa, Iowa State, Minnesota and Penn State — and four are one-time winner's — Cornell College (1947), Iowa Teachers College (now University of Northern Iowa) (1950), Michigan State (1967), and Arizona State (1988).

In 1947 there was only one division of collegiate wrestling, with 102 member

Cover of the official 1947 NCAA program

schools, but many of those did not compete in the NCAA championship. For the most part, teams wrestled only within their conferences. Some conferences restricted NCAA participation to conference winners or high placers, and few schools took a full team. Often coaches were already into their spring sports coaching schedule and could not afford the time. And participation always depended on where the meet was held.

Scott's predecessor, longtime Cornell College coach Dick Barker, who was then in the publishing business in State College, Pennsylvania, brought the Penn State contingent to the tournament in the absence of its coach, Charlie Speidel, who was ill.

The 1947 meet was hosted by the University of Illinois, March 28–29, at the George Huff Gymnasium in Champaign-Urbana, Illinois. The University of Illinois, knowing they would have a strong team, had asked to host the meet. It was the first full-blown championship

The George Huff Gymnasium in Champaign-Urbana, Illinois

since the war, with 112 men representing 31 schools. Only four schools entered full eight-man teams: Illinois, Oklahoma A&M, and the two Iowa schools, Cornell College and Iowa Teachers College. These four, along with Michigan State, were considered the favorites to win the tournament. Tickets for the two-day event cost $2.40; the program was a quarter.

Before the meet began, it was announced that there would be only three defending champions in the meet—Bill Koll, 145 pounds (Iowa Teachers); Bill Courtright, 155 pounds (Michigan); and Dave Shapiro, 165 pounds (Illinois); two champions from 1946 would not be competing: Gerry Leeman and George Dorsch.

Gerry Leeman (Iowa Teachers) was unable to wrestle due to a torn rib cartilage. Harold Mott would substitute at 121 pounds, with Russ Bush at 128 pounds. Teachers would not enter a wrestler at 136 pounds.

George Dorsch, 175 pounds (Oklahoma A&M), had lost a wrestle-off to his freshman teammate, James Gregson. The substitution of Gregson for the defending champion was seen by many as a mistake, in spite of the fact that Gregson had won the wrestle-off before 3,000 A&M fans in Stillwater.

Scott and his eight-man team headed for Illinois on Wednesday, March 26, after working out hard on Monday and Tuesday. It was said that all were in excellent shape except for the station wagon. When they arrived in Champaign-Urbana, the team headed for a hotel. It was essential to have heated rooms—and steamy bathrooms—in order to make weight and rest between bouts.

Scott remembered, "Benny McAdams and I were having lunch with Gus Schrader, the sports editor of the Cedar Rapids *Gazette*, when we noticed water dripping from the ceiling in the main dining room, so I had to get upstairs and shut down the hot water which had overflowed the tub trying to make steam. I think we made a shambles out of the place and the plaster had started to loosen up."

The team worked out on Thursday, with weigh-ins Friday morning. The first or preliminary round was in the afternoon, and the quarter-finals were that evening.

The seeding for the tournament was always important, and no coach was ever completely satisfied with the outcome. Defending champions and outstanding wrestlers were usually seeded, but since Cornell had not fielded a team during the last season, it might be at a disadvantage. On the other hand, the Purple had outstanding records against most of the competition. Scott's only comment was: "We'll be tough and with good luck in the opening rounds we ought to place well up there." This would prove to be the understatement of the year!

Cornell College had one big advantage: it had three "pinners" on the team—Hauser, Snook, and Thomas. A pinner is simply a wrestler who likes to go aggressively for a fall. Coaches love pinners, of course, provided they don't take too much risk. Importantly, each pin scored earned one additional team point. The team scoring system was 6–4–2–1 (six points for a first-place finisher, four points for second place, two for third, and one for fourth); any pin points were added to that total.

The preliminary round—which was watched by only 823 people—went reasonably well. Hauser drew Garth Lappin (Minnesota) and beat him 9–4. Leo Thomsen had a bye. Lowell Lange pinned his man, as did Rodger Snook. Kent Lange lost a tough match to Lager Stecker (Oklahoma) 7–3. Dexter won, and Thomas in a bit of a surprise pinned Ed Ahrens (Iowa Teachers). Al Partin wrestling heavyweight lost to Ray Gunkel (Purdue), a much heavier opponent.

The most egregious example of poor seeding occurred in the 155-pound weight class, when Ken Marlin (Illinois), fourth in NCAA in 1946, upset Jack St. Clair (Oklahoma A&M), runner-up in that same tournament, 9–4. That was the first big blow to Oklahoma A&M's chances.

In the evening quarter-final round, Hauser pinned his man. Then came one of the great bouts of the tournament, albeit a little earlier than expected, which pitted Leo Thomsen against Louis "Lou" Kachiroubas (Illinois) in the 128-pound class. Kachiroubas, a war veteran, had been runner-up to Gerry Leeman at the NCAA the year before and had been defeated by Lowell Lange in the dual meet with Cornell while wrestling up at 136 pounds.

Thomsen seemed headed for one of the tourney's biggest upsets when he built up a 5 to 1 lead in the second period. Kachiroubas, however, worked an arm drag for a takedown just as the period ended. In the final period, Kachiroubas escaped and took Thomsen down for a one-point lead. Thomsen then escaped to tie up the match. Each wrestler rode out the other for the full two minutes of overtime, by which time both men were exhausted. Kachiroubas was awarded the referee's decision for being the more aggressive. Needless to say, the hometown crowd loved it. Lowell Lange believed that Leo had "let the bout get away from him."

Lowell Lange won by decision, Snook pinned his man, and Fred Dexter defeated James Conklin (Indiana) 6–0. The 175-pound weight class—which included Dale Thomas, Glen Brand, Joe Scarpello, James Gregson, and Norman Anthonisen—was perhaps the most competitive. Glen Brand (Iowa State) defeated Dale Thomas 9–2 in a surprisingly lopsided bout. In the other bracket, Joe Scarpello (Iowa) defeated Norman Anthonisen (Illinois) 10–4.

The semi-final round began at 2 P.M. on Saturday. This, of course, was a critical round, determining not only the finalists but also who besides the semifinalists would compete in the final consolation round. Consolation matches were six minutes long, divided into three two-minute periods. Only wrestlers defeated by the two finalists in each weight class were eligible to wrestle in the consolation finals.

Hauser began the proceedings by pinning Arnold Plaza (Purdue), the Big Ten champ who, incidentally, was to win the NCAA title the next two years. At 128 pounds, Kachiroubas advanced, which meant Thomsen would be in the consolation round. Lowell Lange pinned his man, as did Rodger Snook, for his third pin of the tournament.

At 165 pounds, Dexter lost to Jim Eagleton (Oklahoma) 4–1, thus dropping him into the consolations, and Bill Nelson (Iowa Teachers) scored a major upset by edging defending champion David Shapiro (Illinois) 6–5. Shapiro had pinned Nelson in the dual meet.

Glen Brand defeated Robert Klune (Colorado State), assuring Thomas a place in the consolation round. At heavyweight, Richard Hutton (Oklahoma A&M), who had only begun wrestling in the second semester after getting out of the service, scored a narrow last-second victory over Verne Gagne (Minnesota) 2–1.

The first consolation round began in late afternoon. Cornell had three men in the consolations. Thomsen defeated Joe Dickinson (Michigan State) 4–2 in an exact reversal of their dual meet match. This was a big win for Cornell. Fred Dexter edged Bob Wishend (Navy) 2–1, and Dale Thomas defeated Bob Klune.

It had been a long afternoon for everyone but especially for Illinois, which saw its three upper weight class stars, Shapiro, Anthonisen, and Gottfried, defeated. It was a coach's nightmare, a really bad round!

Cornell College had three men in the finals and three now in the third-place consolations. By virtue of a record nine pin points, Cornell had actually clinched the championship, going into the evening finals with an insurmountable lead.

The final consolation round came first in the evening session, and Leo Thomsen defeated McDaniel (Oklahoma A&M) 2–1. Dexter then upset Shapiro 8–6 in another big win for Cornell.

Thomas easily defeated Van Cott (Purdue) 9–4. Thus all three Cornell men had fought back in the consolation round to take third—the mark of a well-balanced team.

The NCAA Finals

There were around 2,500 people in attendance for the finals at Huff Gym, bringing the total attendance for the tournament to some 6,000. By way of comparison, the 2010 NCAA Division I wrestling championship held at the Qwest Center in Omaha, Nebraska, included 330 wrestlers from 77 schools who qualified through their respective conferences. Approximately 95,000 fans were in attendance through six sessions.

Dick Hauser wasted no time disposing of Bill Jernigan (Oklahoma A&M). After a cautious, scoreless first period, with only 34 seconds gone in the second period, Hauser slapped on a head scissors and bar arm, and it was all over. He became the first freshman ever to win a NCAA title, and also the youngest, at age 18 years, 10 months.

In a battle of veterans, Russ Bush (Iowa Teachers) defeated Lou Kachiroubas (Illinois) 4–2, avenging a loss in their dual meet. Bush controlled the match on the mat, and his 2 points riding time made the difference.

Lowell Lange then disposed of Nate Bauer (Oklahoma A&M) 6–3 in his usual workmanlike manner. After giving up a takedown, Lange scored reversals in both the first and second periods and added two points for riding time. He became the second freshman ever to win a NCAA title, and now the youngest, at age 18 years, 7 months. The first three winners were all from West Waterloo High School.

The long-awaited match between Rodger Snook and defending champion Bill Koll (Iowa Teachers) was a bit anticlimactic. Koll used his superior skills on his feet to defeat Snook 7–2. Nonetheless, Snook pinned his way through to the finals and thereby scored as many team points as did Koll.

In the closest bout of the evening, Gale Mikles (Michigan State) defeated the defending champion, Bill Courtright (Michigan), 2–0.

The most exciting bout of the evening was probably that between Bill Nelson (Iowa Teachers), a freshman, and James Eagleton (Oklahoma). For two periods and part of a third, it looked like Eagleton's bout. Then with both men on their feet midway through the third period, Nelson, behind in the scoring, took Eagleton down and pinned him with a "chicken wing" in 7:36.

Joe Scarpello, a freshman wrestling for Iowa under coach Mike Howard, defeated Glen Brand, a sophomore at Iowa State, 10–6. It was Iowa's first title since 1928. These two service veterans were to battle the following year for the NCAA title as well as for the 1948 Olympic team, with Brand coming out on top in both contests. This represented the only significant rivalry between Iowa and Iowa State during the decade. Scarpello went on to win one more NCAA title in 1950.

Oklahoma A&M finally salvaged its sole championship when its freshman heavyweight, Richard Hutton, defeated Ray Gunkel (Purdue)

5–3 with just five seconds left in the overtime.

Thus did Cornell College become the only private college, and with only 415 male students, certainly the smallest, to win the most elusive prize in collegiate wrestling, the NCAA team championship. Cornell College also became the first school outside the state of Oklahoma to win the team title since it was first awarded in 1934.

But there were even more surprises. Iowa colleges accounted for six of the eight champions: Hauser, Bush, Lowell Lange, Koll, Nelson, and Scarpello. All but Koll would be around for the next three years. And five of the champions were freshman—Hauser, Lowell Lange, Nelson, Scarpello, and Hutton—with the latter two being service veterans. Hutton, a graduate of Tulsa Central High School, had served in the military for five years after graduation and had only entered Oklahoma A&M as a freshman in the second semester.

Cornell, scoring 32 points, was awarded the first-place trophy; Iowa Teachers took second with 19 points, and Oklahoma A&M was third with 15 points. Bill Koll was awarded the outstanding wrestler trophy. Art Griffith, the Oklahoma A&M coach, said, "I've coached and watched many of the best teams, but this Cornell bunch sure beats them all."

Cornell won the championship with a well-balanced lineup that yielded two champions, one second, and three third-place finishers out of the eight weight classes. Their aggressive style garnered an unheard-of 10 pin points out of a total of 18.

After the victory, Scott was quoted in the local newspaper as saying rather modestly, "We won the meet because we went out for pins and got them. In a meet like this where most of the boys are good, luck of the draw is important and we were fortunate in drawing opponents we could pin."

The face of collegiate wrestling would never be the same. The win by Cornell and a second by Iowa Teachers represented a realignment among the powerhouses of college wrestling that would eventually result in a new equilibrium between the states of Oklahoma and Iowa.

The Homecoming

According to Rick Meredith, "Students rallied on Sunday to decorate the gym with place cards and paint stores with huge white letters of welcome. Cars formed a line in Lisbon, one mile away, to escort the first contingent of wrestlers into Mount Vernon, where a large crowd had gathered. They had a long wait. The International wagon was tired, and it ran out of juice at Lisbon. We pushed it the last mile to the campus.

"An impromptu meeting was arranged on the gym steps with words of congratulations from President Russell Cole and Dean [Jay B.] MacGregor. Cheers were given as each member of the team stepped from the cars.

"Formal presentation of the trophy was made in a recognition chapel Monday morning. Short talks were given by President Cole, Dean MacGregor, Ivan Blackner, president of the Chamber of Commerce, and Gordon Meredith, team manager."

The only senior on the team, Dale Thomas (center), presents the NCAA wrestling trophy to Cornell President Russell Cole; Coach Scott is at right.

Dale Thomas, who had been selected as honorary captain, made the presentation of the trophy to the school, with faculty representative Mark Hutchinson offering words of acceptance. Then Coach Scott introduced his eight grapplers and expressed appreciation for the fine support that students, faculty, and townspeople had shown during the year.

"Scotty was given praise by each speaker and roars of applause, seldom equaled on the Hill, went up for him and the Purple stalwarts," Meredith exulted.

Waiting for the train: Cornell's NCAA champs head to San Francisco for the NAAU tournament. Back row, from left: Arlo Ellison, Fred Dexter, Dale Thomas, Manager Rick Meredith. Middle row: Coach Scott, Leo Thomsen, Lowell Lange, Kent Lange, Rodger Snook, Al Partin; seated: Dick Hauser, John Gregg.

San Francisco Bound: The National AAU Championship

On the Wednesday morning before the team left for the NCAA championship, the fundraising drive for its next and final trip had kicked off in King Chapel. The Cornell Pep Club, under president Mary Alice Reideker, was sponsoring the campaign to send the team to the National AAU Championship at the Olympic Club in San Francisco on April 11–12. The goal was to raise $2,000 by the following Monday, through contributions from local businesses, townspeople, Cornell students, and nearby alumni, most from Mount Vernon and Cedar Rapids. The $2,000 figure was the amount estimated by Scott to take the starting eight, Meredith, himself, and two other wrestlers by train to California.

President Cole announced that the college would put up one dollar for every three that the student committee contributed, which meant it would contribute $500 if $1,500 were raised. The effort was spearheaded by Scott's friend Al Morrissey, and by Monday half the goal had been met; the balance was raised by Wednesday.

On Saturday morning, April 5, less than a week after the Purple's triumphal return from the NCAA, the entourage boarded the Chicago North West Oriental Limited from Cedar Rapids. They spent two nights on the train, arriving in San Francisco late Monday afternoon in time for a light workout. Scott had allowed for hard workouts on Tuesday and Wednesday and plenty of time for making weight and relaxing before the weigh-ins on Friday. Meredith said, "On the train, I typed several term papers for guys who needed to catch up on studies."

The team stayed at the Turk Street YMCA downtown, which charged $1.00 a night for each wrestler. Uncharacteristically, Scott had made reservations for himself at the St. Francis, one of the most famous hotels in America at that time, right on Union Square and just two blocks from the Olympic Club. It was unusual for Scott to book a room apart from the team, and after a couple of days in San Francisco, a few of the team members took it upon themselves to check up on Scott at the St. Francis. They thought he might be "having a lady friend" up to his room. Scott was not amused.

It is likely that Scott spent time in the bar and dining room. A prime rib dinner from soup to dessert was $5.25; "bar bourbon," Scott's favorite alcoholic beverage, was 50 cents; the room itself was $9 a night.

Unlike the NCAA championship, the NAAU tournament had been held throughout the war years, albeit with somewhat smaller fields. This year the tournament had special appeal since the prestigious Olympic Club was considered one of the finest private clubs in the country. Although there would be many West Coast participants, all of the major East Coast clubs would also be there, together with two partial teams from Oklahoma—Oklahoma A&M and Southwestern Oklahoma Tech (now Southwestern Oklahoma State University)—and several collegiate stars. Conspicuous by its absence was Iowa Teachers, due to budgetary constraints. Cornell, the Oklahoma schools, and the defending champion, the New York Athletic Club (NYAC), were favored to win

The Olympic Club of San Francisco, site of the 1947 NAAU championships

the team title. There were more than 150 entrants in the 10 weight classes, with seven defending national title holders, including Dick Hauser and Lowell Lange. Ticket prices ranged from $.85 to $2.50 per session, with an all-sessions ticket costing $5.00.

The challenge to Cornell's wrestlers was to prove far more difficult than any they had faced to date. First and foremost, there would be no points awarded for pins, which, of course, mitigated their aggressive style. Second, with the scoring system of 5-3-1-1 (points awarded to first through fourth places), Cornell needed to have a few first and second place finishes. In addition, there was always the possibility of poor seeding to worry about.

Scott made some adjustments to his lineup to cover the NAAU's two extra weight classes (115 and 191). He had decided to take John Gregg, a sophomore who could make 115 pounds, and senior Arlo Ellison, 136 pounds, because he had contributed so much in a utility role at weight classes from 136 to 155. He would be in the same weight class as his teammate, Lowell Lange, since a team was allowed more than one competitor in any given weight class.

Scott would move Dexter to 191 pounds and leave heavyweight vacant. Since most heavyweights weighed less than 200 pounds, most would shift to 191 pounds, leaving the heavyweight category to the really big boys. It was a kind of Hobson's choice for competitors: either wrestle a monster at heavyweight or eventually wrestle the great Henry Wittenberg at

191 pounds. Truly one of the finest wrestlers in American history, Wittenberg was to compile a record that was estimated to be 350 wins, with only three losses from 1939 to 1953. His wins included eight NAAU titles, an Olympic gold medal in 1948, and an Olympic silver medal in 1952. He retired in 1953 after winning the Maccabiah Games for the second time.

The first round went well for Cornell. All wrestlers who had matches won.

All those who had second round matches won except for Kent Lange at 155 pounds, who lost a close 1–0 bout to Orville Long of Southwestern Oklahoma Tech and was eliminated. This was an unfortunate seed, since Long went on to win the championship rather easily.

On to the quarter-finals. Due to a smaller field, Gregg at 115 pounds did not wrestle until the quarters. He lost to Leland Christenson (Cal Berkeley), who had been his teammate at Cherokee

Cover of the official 1947 NAAU program

(Iowa) High School. Both had been coached by Roy Garrard in his first coaching job, before taking over for Eriksen at West Waterloo. Hauser, Thomsen, and Lowell Lange advanced. Ellison lost a tough match, 5–3, to Murray Edelman (McBurney YMCA), who had pinned him at the meet in New York City. Snook won by default.

At 165 pounds, Al Partin lost a close 8–7 bout to Jim LaRock (Ithaca YMCA). Partin was at first called the winner of his match, but the decision was later reversed. An official came to the YMCA at 2 A.M. to give Al the bad news. Unfortunately, Scott was not there at the time, since he would most certainly have protested. Partin took this decision in stride and would later be rewarded.

Thomas advanced. Dexter was unceremoniously pinned in 44

seconds by Grover Raines (Oklahoma A&M).

The semi-finals would be the "make or break" round, as it is at most meets. Hauser defeated George Feuerbach (NYAC), a senior at Mepham High School in Bellmore, New York, 2–1. Feuerbach was to go on to win three EIWA titles at Lehigh.

The most interesting weight class was 128 pounds, where Charles Hetrick (Southwestern Oklahoma Tech) scored the first major upset when he pinned Ed Collins, the defending champion for the NYAC.

Lou Kachiroubas (Illinois) advanced to the finals by default when Leo Thomsen failed to make weight. Lowell Lange won by decision after three consecutive pins—pins being somewhat uncharacteristic for him. Snook then defeated Joe Kissane (McBurney YMCA) in a narrow one-point victory. Kissane was the same wrestler who had almost beaten Snook in the meet with McBurney on the Eastern swing. The experience Snook gained in that match proved decisive. Dale Thomas won his match.

Cornell had only Leo Thomsen in the consolation round, and he forfeited his match to Collins for third, failing to make weight again. It made no difference in the point scoring, since both third and fourth places were worth one point.

Thus Cornell College put four men in the finals, while Oklahoma A&M and Southwestern Oklahoma Tech put in two each.

It was a long evening. Everything was running late, since the gym floor at the Olympic Club could accommodate only two mats, and now they were down to one. The final matches were each 12 minutes in duration.

At 115 pounds Grady Penninger (Oklahoma A&M) led things off by besting Christenson (Cal Berkeley) 6–2. Next Hauser, with a 98-straight win streak on the line, wrestled the veteran Charlie Ridenour (NYAC), three-time EIWA champion at Penn Sate, NAAU champ in 1943 at 121 pounds, and winner at 128 pounds the previous year.

The match was even until a flurry of activity near the edge of the mat when both wrestlers rolled under the scorers' table and Ridenour was awarded two points. Scott maintained that neither wrestler had control, but nothing could be done. Hauser lost the match 9–6. This shocked and temporarily demoralized the Cornell contingent.

In the 128-pound championship bout, Charles Hetrick of Southwestern Oklahoma Tech appeared to have won a tight 4–3 decision over Lou Kachiroubas of Illinois on the basis of a 2-point riding time advantage. It was later found that a timer's error had been made and that neither man had riding time, so the bout went to Kachiroubas, who had gained a 3–2 lead with six minutes to go.

Lowell Lange defeated Murray Edelman (McBurney YMCA), 4–1. He was the only man to win both individual national championships— and he was only a freshman!

At 145 pounds it was Cornell vs. Cornell as Rodger Snook wrestled Jimmy Miller (Ithaca YMCA) of Cornell University. Miller was an EIWA champion and defending NAAU champion. Jimmy and his longtime coach and Ithaca wrestling mentor, Bill Layton, had decided at the last minute to drive from Ithaca to San Francisco for the tournament. Along with the LaRock brothers and Bob Kenerson, they drove nonstop in a vintage Packard, arriving with the weigh-in already in progress. "What a drive that was! I don't think I slept for four days," said Miller.

Snook, an outstanding mat wrestler and a dangerous pinner, was said to have the best cradle in the U.S., but he was not as strong from the standing position. Miller, who was good on his feet, knew this, and took full advantage with an unprecedented six takedowns for 12 points. The final score was 15–8. Meredith maintained that Snook was wrestling with a damaged hand, which did not help matters.

At 155 pounds, Long (Southwestern Oklahoma Tech) defeated Newt Copple (wresting unattached, from Lincoln, Nebraska), and at 165 pounds two veterans fought it out, with Doug Lee (Baltimore YMCA) defeating hometown favorite, M. D. "Doc" Northrop, 3–2 (Olympic Club). Dale Thomas now faced Jim Gregson (Oklahoma A&M) at 175 pounds. The outcome could determine who would win the team championship. The score was tied 3–3 with 30 seconds left in the match, when Thomas took Gregson down to win the match 5–3. The Cornell team was elated.

Henry Wittenberg then pinned Grover Rains (Oklahoma A&M) in 1:39 of the first period, the only fall in the finals, thus sealing the deal for Cornell. Ray Gunkel (Purdue) won at heavyweight.

Cornell claimed the team championship with 17 points, Oklahoma A&M trailed at second with 12 points, and Southwestern Oklahoma Tech took third with 11 points. Wittenberg won the outstanding wrestler award. Al Partin won a Longines watch, presented to the wrestler showing the best sportsmanship during the tournament.

It was well after midnight before all the awards were given out. The team went down to the St. Francis Hotel to celebrate, only to find the bar closed, as were all the bars on Powell Street. The celebration would have to wait, but the news had already reached Mount Vernon.

Plaudits and Kudos

A telegram from President Cole to "Cornell Wrestling Team, St. Francis Hotel" read, "Hail to a great wrestling team. Give the boys a victory banquet in Chinatown tonight on me." Unfortunately it was too late for that, too.

Scott himself sent a telegram to his wife, which read, "We won, Lange, Thomas champions, Hauser, Snook second, Thomsen fourth. Tough meet. Love, Scotty."

Russ Newland, sports writer for the San Francisco *Chronicle*, proclaimed Cornell College the "biggest little school in athletics." Scott, along with Meredith and Hauser, had paid a visit to the *Chronicle* offices before the championship began in order to drum up interest in the meet.

Scott prided himself on engendering good sportsmanship in his wrestlers, and the West Waterloo contingent had certainly received good training under both Eriksen and Jarrard. A letter written by John B. Thune, head official at the San Francisco meet, about 10 days after the event, complimented the team on its exemplary demeanor:

President, Cornell College

Mount Vernon, Iowa

Dear Sir,

As head referee of the recent national AAU wrestling tournament held in San Francisco, I wish to commend the Cornell College team and especially its coach for their very fine display of sportsmanship throughout the tournament.

Your team not only won first place by the total number of points, but in the minds of the eight referees and spectators, your coach and team are number one also in the fine points of good ethics in the sport of wrestling.

Sincerely yours,

John B. Thune

On April 16 Iowa Teachers coach Dave McCuskey wrote Scott this letter, which illustrates the respect one man had for the other:

Dear Scotty,

Congratulations on your winning of the National AAU and the NCAA and the season as a whole.

Too bad Dick was outpointed in the finals. He's a fine fellow and a great wrestler and I'm willing to bet he'd win from Ridenour 9 out of 10 times.

You have a great bunch of men and have done an outstanding job of coaching.

The attitude of our fans does not always indicate

the way they really feel. I've heard several of the more rabid ones bemoaning the fact that Dick lost a match. Last winter when the heat was on they felt different about it. Guess we can be grateful that we have fans who are that interested.

At any rate we have enjoyed the competition with your team and wish you the best of luck in the future.

If you have any dope on Olympic Style of Wrestling or anything else pertaining to wrestling, send it to me so that I can get it in the bulletin. In fact, it is essential that I have an article of some kind from you.

Perhaps you can tell us how you get all those falls. You certainly surprised everyone the way you went after falls and got them.

See you after the track meet Saturday.

Cordially,

Dave

Congratulations poured in from across the nation, since the wrestling community appreciated the significance of what the Cornell wrestlers had done: they had now accomplished the incredible feat of winning both national championships in the same year. It would be repeated only once in the postwar period, in 1950, by the powerful Iowa Teachers team. In amateur wrestling, this rarity was equivalent to achieving the Grand Slam in tennis or horse racing's Triple Crown. Yet those are really individual events, while Cornell's was truly a team championship. Perhaps a more apt comparison would have been the winning in college basketball of both the NIT (National Invitational Tournament) and the NCAA championship back in the 1940s and 1950s, when the NIT was actually the more prestigious event. Only the City College of New York accomplished that feat, in 1950, defeating Bradley University of Peoria, Illinois, in Madison Square Garden in both tournaments.

The Celebration

The Cornell team left San Francisco on Sunday on the Overland Limited, which had a scheduled stop at Cedar Rapids at 9:20 A.M. Tuesday, April 15. It also had a special stop planned at Mount Vernon at 10:30 A.M., where an estimated 1,500 townspeople and college students would be waiting in the rain. Unfortunately, the train did not reach Mount Vernon until 11:50 A.M., but the assembled multitude gave Paul Scott and his "Grand Slam" champions a wild, if soggy, welcome.

According to Meredith, as the wrestlers disembarked, the Cornell College band struck up the Cornell victory song, and cheerleaders led the bedraggled assemblage in school yells while President Cole, Bob Hawthorne, president of the student body, and Mount Vernon Mayor John Gaston ran forward to offer formal congratulations.

Among the first off the train were Dale Thomas and Fred Dexter,

Once again, the Cornell College wrestling team returns home triumphant. Just off the train are, from left: Dale Thomas, Leo Thomsen, Lowell Lange, Arlo Ellison, Fred Dexter (holding NAAU trophy), John Gregg, Dick Hauser, Manager Gordon Meredith, Rodger Snook, Al Partin, Kent Lange, Coach Scott.

clutching the championship trophy. Coeds, led by a hastily chosen "Queen of the Wrestlers," Kay Brusso, surrounded the squad members and Coach Scott to reward them with kisses.

A red convertible with President Cole at the wheel led the procession through town to the campus. Scott, his wife, son Richard, and Queen Brusso were his passengers. Trailing along in the downpour were decorated cars bearing the wrestlers. The Mount Vernon fire truck and dozens of private vehicles followed the celebrants.

Cornell President Cole sits in the front seat of the car leading the procession. Wrestling queen Kay Brusso shares the back seat with Paul Scott, his son Richard, and his wife Betty.

Inside the King Chapel, President Cole, Hawthorne, and Ivan Blackner, president of the Mount Vernon Chamber of Commerce, gave the official welcoming address and introduced the wrestlers individually, while hundreds of listeners gathered outside the chapel. Coach Scott then formally presented the championship trophy to the college.

Radio station KCBC Des Moines recorded a 15-minute broadcast of the celebration, and a *Life* magazine photographer was on hand to take pictures. *Life* was the nation's most popular magazine, with a circulation of more than 12 million at its peak. As it turned out, the *Life*

The victory parade passes Mount Vernon storefronts bedecked with congratulatory messages.

article had to wait; it was not published until February 23, 1948. There was, however, a good reason for that.

April 15, 1947, was also opening day in major league baseball, and this date would prove to be the most important in the history of the sport. Jackie Robinson, the first African-American to play in the major leagues, made his debut for the Brooklyn Dodgers at Ebbets Field in Brooklyn. That was clearly the most significant sports event of 1947 and maybe the decade. The next most important was the compilation of victories by the Cornell College wrestling team.

Town and gown turn out in droves to congratulate the wrestlers.

Scott was quoted as saying, "No one can dispute our claim to the best wrestling team in the country. Next year will be better yet."

The Banquet

More than 250 people gathered in Bowman Hall to honor Cornell's championship wrestling team. The dinner was sponsored by the Mount Vernon Chamber of Commerce. Everyone was invited, and tickets, which were $2.00, were sold at several local establishments including Bauman's Store (which is still at its original location). The banquet cost $1.00 per person, with the balance used to pay for guests, including the wrestling team, coach, sports writers, radio announcers, and the speaker.

The principal speaker was none other than Kenneth L. "Tug" Wilson, commissioner of athletics for the Big Ten Conference and vice president of the Olympic committee, the very same individual who had had to override himself in the "Martin incident" and who had permitted the Thomas transfer.

Wilson paid tribute to "a great wrestling team from a great little college." He called the team's achievement "one of the most remarkable in collegiate history," winning not only the NCAA championship but the NAAU championship as well. He continued, "You have defeated men

The 1947 Cornell College Team with NAAU and NCAA championship trophies. Standing, from left: Manager Gordon "Rick" Meredith, John Gregg, Lowell Lange, Arlo Ellison, Leo Thomsen, Richard Hauser, Coach Paul Scott. Kneeling, from left: Rodger Snook, Fred Dexter, Dale Thomas, Al Partin, Kent Lange.

from big schools, schools of 20,000 and 25,000 students. You have been in tough competition and you are to be congratulated." He mentioned particularly their skill, aggressiveness, and sportsmanship.

Paul Scott introduced his team and presented a recording of the Lehigh-Cornell match. Scott also announced that the honorary captain of the team, elected by his teammates, was the only senior on the squad, Dale Thomas.

President Cole and Dr. C. Ward Macy of Coe College, Midwest Conference athletic commissioner, gave short speeches.

Already, the audience was eagerly anticipating the next wrestling season.

The Sequels

The Long Season (1948)

Scott was optimistic that 1948 could be a repeat of 1947. He would have all his starters back save for Dale Thomas, who was graduating along with Ellison and Littell, and they would all have a year's experience under their belts. In addition, Dick Hauser, Lowell Lange, and possibly Leo Thomsen would have a good shot at making the 1948 Olympic team, along with several other wrestlers from Iowa colleges.

Harold "Hek" Kenney, the University of Illinois wrestling coach, had unknowingly done Scott a huge favor by hosting the NCAA championship at Champaign-Urbana. No sooner was the 1947 wrestling season over than Scott, with a great story to tell, was busy recruiting aggressively in Illinois, taking full advantage of the Cornell reputation. He wasted no time signing up three boys from Tilden Tech in Chicago, a tough, inner city powerhouse—Walter Romanowski, Ray Foy, and Bob Weick—plus the two-time Iowa high school champion Harry Horn (one of the five boys Scott took to New York in 1946), and Ralph Samson from Des Moines. Also incoming were the Salisbury twins, James and John, lightweights from Elgin, Illinois. Scott particularly liked the fact that Mr.

Salisbury owned a car dealership in Elgin, which might give him access to a vehicle to replace the aged and infirm International.

The season began before the Christmas break, with a warm-up meet against Beloit, which the Purple won 29–3. Next, as promised, Scott was to take the boys to New Orleans to wrestle the New Orleans Athletic Club, departing on December 27. The hook was that they would attend the Sugar Bowl the day after the meet.

They used two cars, a DeSoto station wagon newly acquired from the Salisbury car dealership, and Scott's 1945 Mercury. Scott's wife and son were also going along. On the way out of town, the axle on the Mercury broke. Fortunately, they found a service station that was able to replace it in a few hours.

Scott's family had ancestors who had served in the military as far back as the Civil War. Scott's grandfather, serving in the 24th Iowa Infantry of the Union Army, had fought and was slightly wounded at Champion Hill, the precursor to Vicksburg. So of course the caravan stopped at Vicksburg to see the battlefield.

The boys were told they would be put up at the New Orleans Athletic Club. What they had not been told was that they would be housed in the trainer's room, where they would have the option of sleeping on a training table or the floor. Richard and Betty were housed in a local B&B whose proprietors practiced voodoo, and the coach found a bed at the club.

Things were fairly relaxed as everyone was wrestling up a weight class. The score of the dual meet was 33–0, with only one close bout.

After returning to Mount Vernon, the team next made a five-day western swing by train. The first match was at the University of Nebraska in Lincoln, where the Purple won 28–0, followed by a long train ride to Denver and wins over Colorado College in Colorado Springs 38–0, Denver University 38–0, Colorado A&M in Fort Collins 24–6, and the

University of Wyoming at Larimie 26–0. They lost only two matches on the entire trip.

The first big dual meet of the season, on January 24, was against the University of Illinois at Champaign-Urbana. Cornell won by a score of 17–9. Rodger Snook lost the first dual meet of his career 2–1, in a match that involved a considerable amount of stalling on the part of the Illinois wrestler, Ken Marlin.

"Scotty sweat blood over the meet," said Norma Morrissey. "The biggest surprise was Rodger Snook's defeat. Snook is the best pinner in the country, but he isn't strong on his feet. So this boy wrestled him smart, and after he was able to go behind Rodger once, for two points, Rodger then got right away for one point; the fellow simply stayed away and won. We felt bad about it. It was the first match Rodger had lost in a dual meet since he was a sophomore in high school. I guess he's been upset about it all this week. The reason Scotty thought he was going to lose for sure when Snook got beat, was because he knew he had to lose heavyweight and thought it would be a pin for Illinois. So in Dexter's [175-pound] match, he got himself in a peck of trouble and was nearly pinned. He made a comeback and got a decision after all. But it was close."

Cornell's record was now 8 and 0.

Norma Morrissey remembers, "A *Life* photographer spent Monday and Tuesday here. He was also at the Illinois-Cornell meet last Saturday. He thinks the pictures have a good chance of getting in, and said to watch for them in the February 6 or 13 issue."

The *Life* magazine article finally appeared in the February 23, 1948, issue. It was a three-page spread and featured photos of the team and a practice session in the wrestling room. It highlighted the dual meet with Illinois, including some great action shots of both Dick Hauser and Leo Thomsen. The school could not have asked for a better piece of publicity for its wrestling program.

The Crash

Before the big feature story appeared in *Life* magazine, however, two of Scott's wrestling stars were involved in an automobile accident that was to change the rest of the season profoundly. In fact, the crash would have an impact on the history of the entire sport.

The crash occurred at 5:15 P.M. on Saturday, January 30, six miles west of Mount Vernon on U.S. Highway 30. Six Cornell College students were injured, some seriously, in a collision with two cars, one towed by the other, driven by Roosevelt Covington of Omaha, who was also seriously injured. The students were on their way back to campus from Cedar Rapids; Hauser was driving the car, which belonged to Kent Lange who was not in the car. The head-on collision occurred when Covington's car came toward them driving on the wrong side of the road.

Hauser said he saw the other car just before the cars hit. The next thing Hauser remembered was that he and Lowell Lange were walking around in a daze. Apparently, both were thrown out of the car, Hauser on one side and Lange on the other. The passenger most seriously injured was Molly Nishoyama, a senior homecoming queen, who was seated between Hauser and Lange. The two coeds sitting in the back seat were not as badly injured, but Buford Beck, the wrestling team manager sitting between them, was. All but one were taken to St. Luke's Hospital in Cedar Rapids. Scott, along with family members in the area, went there as soon as he heard the news.

Hauser had suffered a fracture of a small bone in his right ankle plus cuts and bruises. He was released from the hospital on Wednesday with a cast on his ankle and was sent home for a few days. Lowell Lange was more seriously injured, having suffered a fractured vertebrae and a punctured kidney. He was discharged by the end of the week. Both were expected to make a complete recovery over time, but Lange was not expected to wrestle again that season.

Scott now had some serious decisions to make. First, he needed to come up with a new starting lineup for the remaining dual meets; second, he had to decide what to do about the NCAA and NAAU tournaments, since the team was the defending champion. In addition, both tournaments were qualifiers for the Olympic trials. The 1948 Olympics held particular significance, inasmuch as they were to be the first games held since 1936.

There were four dual meets remaining—an easy one with Grinnell followed by three really tough matches with Southwestern Oklahoma Tech, Michigan State, and Iowa Teachers, all at home. Grinnell was defeated 21–11, with Scott introducing several new men to the lineup, including Richard Small.

Things went downhill from there. It addition to the loss of Dick Hauser and Lowell Lange, Fred Dexter was declared ineligible for collegiate competition. Although eligible by Midwest Conference standards, he did not meet the higher Cornell College "quality point" test. He would, however, be permitted to compete in the National AAU Championship and in Olympic trials later in the season. To make matters worse, two backups, Ben McAdams and Ben Conner, were also out, Conner for the season with a rib injury and McAdams with an undiagnosed illness.

Scott then announced the difficult decision that he would forgo the defense of the NCAA title in favor of concentrating on the NAAU meet, which would be held at Hofstra College on Long Island, New York, April 16–17. Scott felt that he would have a chance of successfully defending the NAAU title because it came much later in the season and would give his injured warriors more time to heal. It was one of the hardest decisions he ever made, since skipping the NCAA deprived four of his remaining starters—Thomsen, Snook, Kent Lange, and Al Partin—an opportunity to compete.

The upcoming Olympics also played into Scott's decision. The first four place finishers in each weight class in both national tournaments, plus the regional Olympic trial qualifiers, would compete in the Olympic trials in Ames, Iowa, at the end of April. The men who qualified by placing in the NCAA meet would probably not wrestle again in the NAAU championship. Obviously, Cornell would have a better chance for the team shot in the NAAU meet if the whole team was competing.

Lowell Lange was back on campus, and Hauser's cast was to be removed, so it was thought that the two could begin working out about March 1. In truth, Lange should not have wrestled for the remainder of the season. His injuries were too severe, and his conditioning never fully recovered. Hauser's case was less obvious, but he certainly was not able to bring himself back to his previous high performance level.

Leo Thomsen, who had a lot of difficulty making weight, immediately moved up to Lowell Lange's spot at 136 pounds.

The last three meets were a disaster. Cornell was crushed by Southwestern Oklahoma Tech 24–6, followed by a loss to Michigan State 25–3, a team the Purple had never lost to in six meetings.

The unkindest cut of all came when they were shut out 28–0 by Teachers at home, before a standing-room-only crowd. It was the first time they had been shut out since 1937. The toughest bout was at 136 pounds, where Russ Bush defeated Leo Thomsen 8–4. Bob Siddens, in his first varsity meet for Teachers, defeated Richard Small at 165 pounds. It was a tough way to end the dual meet season.

The NCAA championship was held at Lehigh University, and Paul Scott attended. According to historian Jay Hammond, "The competition was a qualifier for the 1948 Olympic Trials and used Olympic weight classes and rules, including touch falls and a round-robin bracketing system, which caused considerable confusion among the officials not familiar with the bracketing and bad mark system. A wrestler was eliminated from competition when he accumulated five bad marks. A wrestler received no bad marks if he won by fall, one for a win by decision, and three for a loss either by decision or fall."

With Cornell not entered, the favorite teams were Oklahoma State and Iowa Teachers. Oklahoma State ran away with the team race since Teachers' Russ Bush was declared ineligible, Bill Nelson was forced to medically default, and Gerry Leeman was the victim of a touch fall. Only Bill Koll of Teachers came through, with five consecutive pins to win his weight class and the Outstanding Wrestler Award for the second consecutive year; he was the first wrestler ever to win the award twice. The "Teachers curse" persisted.

Post Season

Scott first sent some of his men to the State AAU meet in Fort Dodge, where he could wrestle any of his squad, including freshmen. Several of them did well including Hauser, Walter Romanowski, Kent Lange, Rodger Snook, Al Partin, Fred Dexter, and Harry Horn. Lowell Lange did not participate.

Next, Scott sent his men to two of the regional Olympic try-out locations, where the first two men in each weight class would qualify. Hauser, Thomsen, Kent Lange, Al Partin, Fred Dexter, and Ralph Samson went to Cedar Falls, and Walt Romanoski, Lowell Lange, Rodger Snook, and Harry Horn went to Omaha.

All of them qualified for the final trials except Leo Thomsen and Kent Lange. They would have one last chance to qualify—the NAAU Tournament in Hempstead, New York.

1948 NAAU Championship

Scott took his largest contingent ever—12 wrestlers in all—to the NAAU meet in Hempstead, where Cornell was the defending champion. Four vehicles were used including the International, which had to be resurrected to make the trip. The International passengers had to dodge leaks in the roof, but this time it was the Salisbury car that had problems: first a flat tire and then a stall-out due to rain. They first stayed at the Sloane House YMCA in New York City and visited such attractions as Times Square, Radio City with its world-famous Rockettes chorus line, the Empire State Building, and the Statue of Liberty. During the meet the team stayed at the Nautilus Club, a summer resort on the South Shore of Long Island.

Leo Thomsen proved to be the surprise of the meet when he won the 136.5-pound class with a 2–1 victory in the finals against Elias George of Oklahoma A&M. Fred Dexter, wrestling unattached, took third place at 174. Kent Lange took second defeating Jimmy Miller, by then the Cornell University coach, 3–0 at 147.5, before losing to veteran Newt Copple. Rodger Snook took fourth. Cornell graduate Dale Thomas

Program cover of 1948 U. S. Olympic Team Trials

successfully defended the 174-pound title he had won in San Francisco the year before. Hauser and Lowell Lange both failed to place, Lange losing to teammate Thomsen in the semifinal round 2–1. Cornell nonetheless tied for third place with the NYAC; Navy came in first and Oklahoma A&M second. Teachers did not participate.

1948 Olympics

Ten Cornell College men had qualified for the final Olympic tryouts, to be held at Iowa State College in Ames on April 29, 30, and May 1. Iowa Teachers also had 10 qualifiers, and Oklahoma A&M led the field with 16. Bill Koll and Henry Wittenberg were the only odds-on favorites to make the team.

Hauser and Lowell Lange failed to place, but Leo Thomsen had an outstanding tournament and reached the finals against Hal Moore

(Oklahoma A&M) at 136.5. He had wrestled another 15-minute match earlier, while Moore had a bye. Wrestling with a badly bruised ear, Thomsen lost a close 2–1 split decision in the 15-minute finals and became the Olympic alternate. It was somewhat surprising that the least likely of the West Waterloo trio was the one who made the team, but the tradition remained unbroken: tiny Cornell College had placed a man on every Olympic team since 1924. Iowa Teachers put three men on the team — Gerry Leeman, Bill Koll, and Bill Nelson. The Iowans had hoped that either Dave McCuskey or Paul Scott would be appointed team coach, but that honor went to Art Griffith of Oklahoma A&M. Cliff Keen, another of Ed Gallagher's protégé's, was the team manager.

After the trials in Ames, 16 wrestlers emerged as members of the U.S. 1948 Olympic team. Seated, from left: Gerald Leeman (Iowa Teachers), Hal Moore (Oklahoma A&M), William Koll (Iowa Teachers), William Nelson (Iowa Teachers), Glenn Brand (Iowa State), and Henry Wittenberg (New York Police Association). Standing, from left: William Jernigan (Oklahoma A&M), Leland Christensen (University of California), Malcolm MacDonald (Navy); Leo Thomsen (Cornell College), John Fletcher (Navy), Leland Merrill (NYAC), Joe Scarpello (University of Iowa), Verne Gagne (University of Minnesota), Robert Maldegan (Michigan State), and Richard Hutton (Oklahoma A&M).

There were meant to be wrestle-offs between the winners of each weight class and their alternates, but in the case of Leo Thomsen this never happened. In this instance it was believed by the Iowans that Griffith's bias clearly showed.

After a 12-year moratorium, the Olympic Games were held in London in the summer of 1948. The U.S. team did well, with Glen Brand and Henry Wittenberg both winning gold medals, and Gerry Leeman winning a silver medal. (Brand was quoted as saying that had his archrival, Iowa's Joe Scarpello, wrestled, he too would have won a gold medal.) Leland Merrill, wrestling in place of Bill Nelson, who was injured in training, took the bronze medal. Bill Koll, who was a victim of the arcane Olympic scoring system, placed fifth. Hal Moore placed sixth. Dick Hutton, the heavyweight, was injured in one of his bouts and placed seventh.

Redemption (1949)

After a successful cross-country season in the fall of 1948, Scott was looking forward to another full wrestling schedule. The Waterloo trio was back, with Hauser and Lowell Lange seemingly healed from their automobile accident. The team would also add the two outstanding freshmen from the previous season, Walter "Mouse" Romanowski and Bill "Chico" Nardini.

The first four meets were no contests, with Cornell winning handily over Beloit, St. Ambrose, Augustana, and Grinnell. The Purple then lost a close one to Michigan State 15–13, followed by easy wins over Colorado State and Bradley. They narrowly beat Nebraska 14–12, then crushed Southwestern Oklahoma State and Kansas State.

The big dual meet with Iowa Teachers would be the last of the season, held in Cedar Falls with an estimated 4,000 eager fans looking on. Through most of the season everyone had been wrestling up one weight class, and Scott decided to leave it that way, except for Walter Romanowski, who dropped to 121 pounds. He lost a close match to John

Harrison 7–5. Hauser then tied it up with a 6–4 decision over Luverne Klar at 128 Pounds. Russ Bush and Leo Thomsen wrestled to a 3–3 draw.

In an unprecedented maneuver, Scott had both Lange brothers weigh in at 145 pounds. He decided to wrestle Kent Lange against Bob Siddens, the Teachers utility man, who had wrestled anywhere from 145 to 175 pounds during the season. Kent won the match 4–0. Scott then moved brother Lowell up to 155 pounds to challenge the new Teachers star Keith Young, who had succeeded Bill Koll. Spotting Young 10 pounds, Lange lost a close 4–2 bout. It was the first and only loss of his collegiate career.

Teachers won the rest of the bouts easily. Rodger Snook, who had moved up two weight classes to 165 pounds, lost to Bill Smith 8–3. Bill Nelson outpointed Al Partin 4–0 at 175 pounds, and heavyweight Fred Stoeker defeated Fred Dexter 5–2.

The final score was 17–8 in favor of Teachers. Cornell's season dual meet record was nine wins and two losses.

Cornell won the Midwest Conference easily, with Richard Small winning the 165-pound class. It was to be the high point of his college career. Small was to become the largest donor to Cornell in the history of the college as well as a significant contributor to important wrestling institutions.

The 1949 NCAA championship was held at Colorado A&M in Fort Collins, Colorado. The favored team was Oklahoma A&M, with Iowa Teachers and Cornell College also in contention.

In a semifinal match-up of the NCAA champions for the past two seasons at 121 pounds, Arnold Plaza of Purdue edged Dick Hauser 4–3. Hauser won his consolation match for third place by pinning Garth Lappin (Minnesota) in 6:40, while Plaza went on to win the title.

In the finals at 128 pounds Charlie Hetrick (Southwestern Oklahoma Tech) upset Thomsen 4–1 after escaping and scoring a takedown in the second period and then riding Thomsen for most of the third period. Hetrick had beaten Russ Bush, a previous champion, 4–2 in the semifinals,.

Lowell Lange then cut through the 136-pound weight class with two pins and no points scored again him. He easily regained his title of two years earlier by defeating defending champion Dick Dickenson (Michigan State) 6–0, scoring an early takedown and controlling his opponent for the entire match.

Kent Lange wrestled exceptionally well, losing a tough 7–5 match to Keith Young (Iowa Teachers) in one of the semifinals. Lange went on to place third, while Young won the weight class, following in the footsteps of Bill Koll.

Nelson won, and Rodger Snook placed fourth at 155 pounds. Bill Smith at 165 pounds also won for Teachers.

The heavyweight championship was one of the most controversial matches in wrestling history. The contest between Verne Gagne (Minnesota) and the two-time defending champion Dick Hutton (Oklahoma State) ended in a tie in regulation. Finn Eriksen, one of the most respected referees in the game, declared Gagne the winner by referee's decision on the basis of a slim amount (less than one minute) of riding time. Hutton had chased Gagne all over the mat in the final period and was very close to scoring a takedown at the buzzer, but he apparently did not have control. Oklahoma State coach Art Griffith felt that it was a "great injustice." It proved to be the only loss of Hutton's entire career and ultimately deprived him of being the first four-time champion, since he was to win again in 1950.

With great team balance, Oklahoma State won the team championship yet again, with 32 points to Iowa Teachers' 27. Teachers once again had three champions. Cornell was a respectable third with 22 points.

Charles Hetrick was awarded the Most Outstanding Wrestler trophy over Lowell Lange on the basis of his wins over Bush and Thomsen.

Lowell Lange did nothing more than run through the tournament without giving up a single point and defeating the defending champion soundly! This was one of the biggest disappointments of his career, along with not making the Olympic team due to injury.

Next was the National AAU Tournament, held at Coe College in Cedar Rapids, Iowa. It turned out to be a three-way race between Teachers, Cornell, and the defending champion, Navy.

Hauser and Romanowski both entered the 128-pound class; Hauser lost a tough 1–0 final to Bush, and Romanowski took fourth. Lowell Lange and Leo Thomsen both entered the 135-pound class, and Lange defeated Thomsen in the final, 2–1. Keith Young won again at 145 pounds, and Kent Lange defeated Rodger Snook 2–0 for third and fourth places.

Teachers' Nelson and Smith won again. Smith's win was a tough 10–7 decision against Jim LaRock (Ithaca College), with whom he would continue to battle at NAAU tournaments and at the Olympic trials in 1952. In the 175-pound weight class, Fred Dexter won a referee's decision, while Al Partin lost to the eventual champion, Shuford Swift (Navy) in the semi-final round. Swift pinned Dexter in the finals, and Partin took third.

Heavyweight Henry Wittenberg was unable to defend his 191-pound title, which he had won for the past seven years. As a policeman in New York City, which was then beset by a taxicab strike, he was required to remain on duty. Verne Gagne won the 191-pound final on a referee's decision.

With Young, Nelson, and Smith winning again, Cornell College lost the team championship to Teachers 37–32.

Cornell was definitively back and would doubtless be battling it out with Oklahoma State and Iowa Teachers again next year.

The Final Season (1950)

Cornell's wrestling season began with a 15–9 win over Nebraska in Lincoln at the start of the team's western swing, where the Purple defeated

Colorado State University and then won a surprisingly close match 16–13 against Wyoming. Several easy wins over Augustana, Knox, University of Denver, St. Ambrose, and Arkansas State were followed by a close 14–12 win over Michigan State. They then defeated Grinnell College in preparation for the big finale against Teachers. Cornell was 10–0.

The dual meet with Teachers, the climax of a thunderous all-day pep rally and parade, was held at Cornell's Alumni Gym on March 10, 1950. A capacity-stretching crowd of more than 1,200 was in attendance, some having lined up for entrance five hours before the meet started. This was the last home appearance of Scott's graduating seniors, the Magnificent Seven: Hauser, Thomsen, both Langes, Snook, Dexter, and Partin (now 28 years old and known as the "grand old man of wrestling").

Scott's only hope for victory would be for the Waterloo trio to get the team off to a good start, hopefully winning all their matches. He asked them all to cut to their lower weights one last time. All three had been wrestling up a weight class for most of the season.

Unfortunately, things did not go well. Hauser came out aggressively against Frank Altman and established an early lead, but the match ended in a 7–7 score, with Altman winning with one point riding time. It was Hauser's first collegiate dual meet loss and his first dual meet loss since his freshman year in high school.

Thomsen got the lead in his match with Luverne Klar 6–4 at the end of the second period, but the match eventually ended in an 8–8 draw. Both Hauser and Thomsen were clearly feeling the effects of cutting weight.

Lowell Lange defeated Floyd Oglesby 9–4, and Rodger Snook easily defeated Clyde Bean 4–0. Teachers then dominated the last four matches as Keith Young defeated Kent Lange at 155 pounds 7–1; Bill Nelson decisioned Bill Nardini at 165 pounds 7–1; Bill Smith defeated Fred Dexter 7–0 at 175 pounds; and Fred Stoeker decimated Al Partin 7–0. Teachers won the meet 17–8. In hindsight, this marked the end of the first great dual meet rivalry in Iowa collegiate wrestling history. No fewer than 11 wrestlers had either won or placed in the NCAA and NAAU tournaments in the previous three years. These included the seven Cornell College starters plus Teachers stars Keith Young, Bill Nelson, and Bill Smith, and Luverne Klar.

In the Midwest Conference tournament, Cornell again crushed its opponents.

1950 NCAA Championship

The 1950 NCAA championship was held on the Iowa Teachers campus in Cedar Falls. Teachers and Oklahoma A&M were the clear favorites. The tournament was held on March 24 and 25.

Cornell was devastated when Hauser for the first time in his career failed to make weight, by a half pound. Cutting weight had become increasingly difficult and had finally caught up with him; the young man who won the NCAA championship as a freshman saw his career end at the weigh-in. It was a frustrating finish to one of the most sensational scholastic wrestling careers of all time.

Romanowski made it to the finals with an upset win 4–2 over Charles Hetrick, the defending champion from Southwestern Oklahoma Tech. He let the final slip away from him in the final second to Joseph Patacsil of Purdue by a score of 3–2.

Lowell Lange wrestled well in spite of coming down with the flu. In the finals he barely won a referee's decision over Lloyd Oglesby of Teachers after the two had wrestled to a 2–2 tie. Lange had beaten Oglesby badly in the dual meet a few weeks before.

This was Lowell Lange's third NCAA title. Had it not been for the car crash, it's almost certain that he would have been the first wrestler to win four titles. Rodger Snook and Bill Nardini both took fourth for Cornell.

This was Teachers' year as Young, Nelson, and Smith all won

again. Keith Young went on to win his third title in 1951, thus giving Teachers unprecedented, back-to-back, three-time champions in the same weight class, with Koll and Young each winning three titles at 145 pounds.

Joe Scarpello (Iowa) won his second title at 175 pounds, and Dick Hutton (Oklahoma A&M) won his third title, with a referee's decision over Fred Stoeker (Teachers). Scarpello, Iowa's first four-time All-American, became at age 27 years, 3 months the oldest NCAA champion to that point, with Hutton second-oldest at 26 years, 8 months.

Thus, Iowa Teachers finally won the NCAA championship they had been seeking since 1946. Purdue was second with 16 points, followed by Cornell with 14. Had Hauser made weight, Cornell would undoubtedly have been second. Oklahoma A&M had a poor showing and finished fourth.

According to Jay Hammond, "Teachers ended five years of frustration by finishing first with 30 points and three individual titles. It was the fourth time in five seasons that they had crowned three champions."

Many of the heavier-weight wrestlers of the post-war period entered the professional wrestling arena, including Verne Gagne, Joe Scarpello, Jim LaRock, Ray Gunkel, Mike DiBiase, and Dick Hutton. Hutton, after another five-year stint of military service, competed for 10 years, winning the heavyweight belt from Lou Thesz in 1957 and holding it for two years. Gagne became a very successful professional wrestler and wrestling promoter, staying involved with the sport for more than 40 years.

Years later, in an interview by Mike Chapman, Paul Scott was asked what he thought would be the legacy of his Cornell program. "I think our successes at Cornell stimulated wrestling at other small colleges in the Midwest. They thought that maybe they could compete on even terms with the big schools in at least one sport."

Summing Up

During the four-year period from 1947 through 1950, tiny Cornell College won two national team championships, including the "grand slam" of wrestling in 1947, and never finished lower than third in any national championship it entered. And the school had once again placed a man on the Olympic team—Leo Thomsen was the alternate at 136.5 pounds in the 1948 games.

Lowell Lange won a total of six national championships—three NCAA titles, and three NAAU titles—plus the NAAU title he won while a senior in high school. Had he not been seriously injured in the car crash in 1948, he most certainly would have been the first man to win four NCAA titles; it is likely he would have won at least one more NAAU title, and there is a strong possibility that he would have won a slot on the 1948 U.S. Olympic team.

Scott said, "Lowell had natural gifts: he had tremendous skill, balance, and anticipation, and he did some things no one else could do on the mat. I think he and Bill Koll were the two greatest wrestler of the 1940s, and two of the greatest wrestlers of all time."

Scott was of the opinion that Hauser had had the ability to compile a record equal to that of another West High product, Dan Gable, who won 181 consecutive matches in high school and college, but the car accident changed all that. Though Hauser came back physically, Scott believed that he never again achieved the mental conditioning that he had possessed prior to the crash. "He had been a terror on the mat, just like Gable in his mental approach to the sport," Scott told historian Mike Chapman, "but I don't think Dick ever reached that peak again after the accident." In the end, every athlete deserves to be remembered for the best that was in him, and when Hauser was at his best, there was nobody better.

All the team members who began wrestling together as freshmen graduated in 1950 after four years. Paul Scott ended his tenure at Cornell with a dual meet record of 55–8–1, having faced some of the toughest teams in the history of the sport. He never coached again.

New Directions

Moving On

After graduation, Dick Hauser and Lowell Lange, along with Bill Smith, Leland Christenson (Los Angeles Athletic Club), and Frank Altman, were invited to make a trip to Japan in late June to wrestle some exhibition matches in Tokyo. En route, they visited Cornell College alums in Los Angeles and toured the 20th Century Fox studios. In Japan they toured several cities including Nagoya, Osaka, Hiroshima, and Nara. Hauser and Lange were reportedly the only undefeated members of the squad.

The graduates were not the only ones leaving Cornell. Scott had become increasingly concerned about the support he was getting from President Cole for the athletic department in general and for the wrestling program in particular. It appeared that although initially enamored with the success of the wrestling team, Cole and some of the faculty members had come to believe that it might reflect poorly on the college if it were considered a "wrestling school." Scott knew that he needed help in the way of scholarships in order to compete with the larger public institutions, with their lower tuitions, lower academic standards, and athletic scholarships. This reality was especially apparent after the first wave of GI Bill recipients had passed through the college system.

The paradox here was that the more successful Scott became with his wrestling team, the more resistant the administration became to the whole enterprise. This bothered Scott to no end and figured heavily in his eventual resignation. In addition, he was getting burned out by having to juggle so many jobs, including athletic director, cross-country and track coach, and of course wrestling coach. Moreover, the extensive travel required, for both away meets and recruiting, was wearing on him. He did not want to leave Cornell before his "boys" graduated in the spring of 1950—but that season would definitely be his last. Scott had seen them through academic difficulties, problems with girlfriends, and scrapes with the law. They had all graduated on schedule. It was time to move on.

Back in the spring of 1949 there had been an opening at Davidson College in Davidson, North Carolina, when the athletic director decided to take the job of head basketball coach at Harvard. Scott was approached then but deferred making a decision. Ultimately, however, he took the job at Davidson, and his resignation was made public over the 1949 Christmas holiday period. He was to assume his new duties after the end of the wrestling season.

In an interview in a local paper, Scott said, "I assure you that only the most attractive of opportunities for my family and myself could have ever caused me to consider leaving Cornell.

"I have been happy here at Cornell and have deemed it a privilege to be a member of its faculty. I have received wonderful treatment from both faculty and administration. We will regret very much leaving the Hilltop and our friends and associates."

Another way of putting it would be the old Kenny Rogers lyrics: "You've got to know when to hold 'em, know when to fold 'em, know when to walk away, and know when to run."

Cornell in Transition

Scott would be a hard man to replace. He had run a three-man athletic department that included eight varsity sports (all men's) as well as junior varsity and freshmen sports. President Cole appointed a search committee consisting of the faculty committee on athletics. By mid-April they had selected 30-year-old Harry J. "Mike" Miller, assistant football and assistant wrestling coach at the University of Nebraska. He would take over the department on July 15. Walt Koch would remain as football and basketball coach. By mid-May it was announced that Jim Fox of Davenport would be the new wrestling coach. A fourth man, Al Duhn, would also be added to the staff. Theses moves were meant to alleviate the heavy coaching assignments of the past few years.

At the year-end athletic banquet, in his final appearance as a Cornell faculty member, Scott paid tribute to all of his athletes and was himself presented with a gold wristwatch from the "C" Club. Scott's successor, Mike Miller, also spoke. And then the Scotts were off to Davidson.

The appointment of Fox fell through, so Miller needed to begin the search for a new wrestling coach all over again. Ed Hitchcock, age 41, a man from Salina, Kansas, with 17 years of coaching experience, was brought to Cornell with his family September 1. He assisted in football before wrestling season began. By all accounts, Hitch, as he was called, was a popular figure on campus.

Wrestling practices began, but soon tragedy struck. On December 4 Hitchcock had a heart attack and died suddenly. Miller and Al Duhn attended his funeral services in Oberlin, Kansas. A memorial service was held the following week in Cornell's King Chapel.

It was then that President Cole and Miller called upon Cornell College's greatest wrestler, Lowell Lange. He had received a one-year military deferment and was a graduate student at the University of Iowa in Iowa City, only a few miles away. Fortunately, Lowell was in excellent shape, since he had been training at the University of Iowa for a wrestling trip to Turkey on December 16, sponsored by the Turkish AAU. Walter Romanowski was another in the group of wrestlers, who were to compete with teams from Iran and Switzerland also. While in New York, the rendezvous point for the trip, "Tiger" Lange appeared on NBC's *Strike It Rich* program. That long-running show featured people facing a financial obstacle who described their plight and appealed to the national TV audience for support; Lange was seeking donations for the wrestlers' trip to Turkey. They returned to the States on December 30.

Lange accepted Cornell's offer of $1,200 to coach the team for the remainder of the season. This would prove to be a wise choice for Cornell. With a lot of new wrestlers to work with, Lange's team went 6–3 with one tie. They again won the Midwest Conference.

At the NCAA championships, Lange saw Walter Romanowski win the 130-pound weight class, defeating Hal Moore, the Olympian from Oklahoma A&M who had previously beaten him 11–6 in the dual meet. For this effort Romanowski—who was to be Cornell's last NCAA champion—was awarded the Outstanding Wrestler trophy. It was the only one ever awarded to a Cornell College wrestler, and the prize that had eluded Lange himself. After the wrestling season, Lange began his military service.

His replacement was none other than Bill Koll, the great star of the Teachers team, who had been coaching at the University of Chicago while working on his master's degree at Northwestern. The Purple went 5 and 3 for the season.

Meanwhile, Teachers made its last challenge to the Oklahoma teams in the 1952 NCAA championship, losing by the narrowest of margins, 22–21, to rising star Oklahoma, with Oklahoma State a close third with 20 points. When Mike Howard finally announced his retirement from the University of Iowa after 31 years, Teacher's coach Dave McCuskey

114

jumped at the opportunity to coach the Hawkeyes. Bill Koll then moved to Teachers to take over for McCuskey and was to remain there for 11 years.

The departures of Scott and then McCuskey coincided with the beginning of the end of the first golden era of Iowa collegiate wrestling. Lloyd Corwin was Cornell's last NCAA Division I place winner, finishing third at 147 pounds in 1954 and second in 1955, when he was pinned in the finals by Lehigh star Ed Eichelberger, coached by Gerry Leeman. Teachers' last NCAA champion of the era was Bill Weick at 157 pounds, coming back from military service in 1955 to regain the crown he first won in 1952.

The Teachers dynasty spanned the years 1946 through 1952 and yielded 15 individual NCAA titles, one NCAA team championship plus four second-place finishes, and two NAAU team championships; it included the "grand slam" in 1950. Teachers also placed three men on the 1948 Olympic team. McCuskey's magic was apparently not transferable; in his 20-year tenure at the University of Iowa, he never won a team championship.

As the use of the GI Bill waned, the smaller powers like Cornell College and Iowa Teachers were no longer able to compete with the large universities and their generous athletic scholarships. Yet it was the rivalry between these two small schools, one private and one public, that had demonstrated that schools outside of Oklahoma could win a national championship.

It was not until 1965 that one of the now major powers in Iowa wrestling won its first NCAA championship, at the University of Wyoming in a blizzard: Iowa State won a stunning come-from-behind victory over Oklahoma State, 87–86. This win was followed by several first and second place finishes through the 1960s and early 1970s. The University of Iowa finally won its first NCAA championship in 1975. From then until the present day, the rivalry between the Iowa and Oklahoma powerhouses has dominated the sport.

The Scotts and Southern Living

After Cornell's academic year ended in the spring of 1950, the Scotts moved to Davidson, North Carolina, in plenty of time to get acclimated and enroll Richard in school. The family was provided an attractive home in the faculty area. Scott's job as director of physical education and athletics came with the title of full professor and a staff of eight coaches plus a full-time secretary. He more than doubled his salary.

Davidson College was a 113-year-old private, Presbyterian, all-male, all-white college with an enrollment of about 1,000 students. The town of Davidson, population 2,000, was located 19 miles north of Charlotte, North Carolina. Scott thought of the relationship between the two towns as similar to that between Mount Vernon and Cedar Rapids.

The college occupied a 50-acre campus and owned an adjacent 65-acre golf course. There were 16 college buildings, including the new state-of-the-art Johnston Memorial Gym. Richardson Field, the athletic stadium, had a capacity of 9,000 with a practice field, baseball diamonds, and tennis courts. Davidson competed in the Southern Conference, usually against much larger schools.

Scott served in his post for four years, and by all accounts he did an outstanding job. In 1952 he was instrumental in conducting the Southeastern U.S. Olympic wrestling team trials at Davidson. However, Scott and his wife were never truly comfortable at Davidson, although they were treated very well. Scott always had a couple of underlying issues with Davidson.

Scott's judgment was that Davidson was a great school educationally, but that its philosophy about athletics—in his words, "We'd rather be beat 40 or 50 points by Georgia Tech than beat Presbyterian [a school closer to Davidson's size] or some other smaller school"—was flawed. The other problem, which Scott articulated only privately, was the matter of race relations in the South, where society was essentially segregated. Although Iowa did not have a large black population during this period, Scott and

Cornell College prided themselves in having an inclusive approach to race relations. Scott may have been a bit naïve about all of this when he arrived in Davidson.

He could never get over the harsh reality he discovered. At one point, he donated some used Davidson football gear to a black team in town. When one of the trustees happened to see the boys playing in what looked like Davidson jerseys, Scott was told that this was "just not done."

Today, Davidson has a 450-acre main campus plus a 106-acre Lake Campus with 1,700 students, 50 percent male and 50 percent female. Students of color represent 14 percent of the enrollment. It ranks among the strongest and most selective of the smaller liberal arts colleges and was the first liberal arts college to eliminate loans in financial aid packages.

When Scott was approached by Cornell to return and take over its alumni association, it was an easy decision. Upon Scott's leaving Davidson, President John R. Cunningham said, "The Davidson college community is distressed to lose Paul Scott and his fine family. It is a compliment that his alma mater insists upon his return as Alumni Secretary. Mr. Scott is a clean-cut Christian gentleman. We shall miss him at Davidson. Our best wishes accompany him on his return to Cornell."

The Tragedy of Rodger Snook

In May 1954, while Scott was still at Davidson, Rodger Snook was severely injured in an automobile accident. Snook, who had thoroughly enjoyed Cornell as a student, had taken a job as a recruiter in the college admissions office in the fall of 1950. He was returning from a recruiting trip when his car was hit head-on by a drunken priest driving on the wrong side of the road. The priest was never prosecuted, since the Roman Catholic Church, with the help of the Iowa State Highway Department, was able to cover up the accident.

Snook remained in a coma at the Veteran's Hospital in Iowa City from May until October. When he finally regained consciousness, he found he was a paraplegic with only limited use of his arms and hands and impaired speech and eyesight. The entire Cornell College community was stunned by the misfortune. Scott, of course, visited him as soon as he returned from Davison and several times thereafter.

Prior to the accident Snook had become engaged and was to be married in September 1954. His fiancée stood by him throughout the ordeal. He was eventually transferred to a Veteran's Hospital near his hometown of Newton, New Jersey, where he continued to attempt his rehabilitation. There was little chance of recovery.

According to his niece, Jane Snook Sattelberg: "He was still a hometown hero. When he attended one of the high school wrestling matches with his father and a nephew, he received a standing ovation when his presence was announced to the crowd."

Snook became severely depressed, and not wishing to be a burden to anyone, he took his own life on May 17, 1956. Scott, who had visited him in New Jersey a few months before his death, was on vacation when he received the news. He was so distraught that he simply could not function for the entire day. Scott truly loved Rodger Snook, as he did all of his team members.

Alumni Director

Meanwhile, back at Cornell College another drama had played out, this time involving the alumni office. Orville Rennie, who had been in charge of the Alumni Association, resigned after seven years in office, during which time the organization had had a contentious relationship with President Cole.

The association, being a quasi-independent body, was permitted to choose its own leader. Its chairman, Clarence O. Pauley '01, was the most influential person in the association at that time. He also served on Cornell's board and was a generous contributor to the college. It was he who persuaded Paul Scott to come back to Cornell. He convinced Scott that he would have enough money to run an effective alumni program, ensured by Pauley's personally underwriting the office for several years.

So the Scotts moved back to Mount Vernon after the 1954 school year ended at Davidson. They enrolled Richard in the eighth grade, and they bought a modest house, the first home that Paul Scott had ever owned, on a shaded street north of the campus. He was to live in this same house for the next 49 years, almost until the day he died. One of the Scotts' proudest moments came when their son and only child graduated from Cornell College in June 1963.

Alumni Director Paul Scott

"Scott directed the alumni office for the next 22 years with tact and enormous energy, thus contributing to the steady improvement of the relationship of the college to its alumni," said President Philip B. Secor, on Scott's retirement.

Under Scott's direction, the annual fund participation went from 10 percent in 1954 to 29 percent in 1964. He more than quadrupled the alumni club program, starting with 30 clubs and growing to 128 clubs. Scott hosted 860 alumni functions in 115 cities. He coordinated alumni activities at all fall homecomings and June alumni weekends for 22 years. Needless to say, the job involved much travel around the country, and everywhere he went he showed color slides, a proclivity for which he was famous.

Scott was a "walking Roladex file" with an uncanny knack for remembering names and faces. He claimed he could identify 1,100 alums and associates, and no one disputed him. Although he stood only five feet four inches tall, Scott possessed an energy and larger-than-life presence that was palpable whenever he walked into a room. His enthusiasm and warmth made a memorable first impression, and he had the ability to make whomever he was speaking with feel uniquely important.

Scott's life was not without personal tragedy. His beloved wife of nearly 35 years, Betty, died in March of 1969 following a long illness. He was remarried in June of 1970 to another Betty (Hanlon) of Mount Vernon, the librarian of the town's elementary school. That summer he and his new bride took an Aegean Sea cruise sponsored by Cornell. Gordon "Rick" Meredith was part of the alumni contingent.

Retirement Dinner

Scott retired as alumni director in the spring of 1976. In what was ostensibly a dinner-dance, 300 friends climaxed Paul Scott Day by giving "Mr. Cornell" a roast, presided over by Charles F. Warden '41, president of the Alumni Association. College presidents, former classmates, trustees, teachers, and associates joined in the roast.

It was announced by President Secor that the Paul K. Scott Outstanding Wrestler of the Year Award was established in his honor, along with the Paul K. Scott Alumni Scholarship Fund, which was created through the donations of more than 1,000 Cornell alumni and friends. These honors recognized Scott's significant achievements in two distinct fields, wrestling and alumni affairs. F. Scott Fitzgerald said in *The Last Tycoon*, "There are no second acts in American lives." Clearly he had never met Paul Scott.

Scott was followed as alumni director by his hand-picked successor, Bob Majors '57. Majors, who wrestled for Cornell College from 1954 through 1957, won the Midwest Conference Championship three times. He joined the development staff in 1966, became development director in 1969, and served as alumni director from 1976 until 1986 when he returned to the development staff as Director of Planned Giving until his retirement in 1999.

Scott in Retirement

Paul Scott thoroughly enjoyed his retirement. He and Betty continued to live in Mount Vernon but spent the winter months, starting the day after Christmas, in Green Valley, Arizona. Scott lived for golf and played almost every day that he could and eventually shot his age. He scored a hole-in-one at the Canoa Hills Golf Course near Green Valley at the age of 84.

In Iowa, Scott played at the Hillcrest Country Club in Mount Vernon and the Lake MacBride Golf Course in Solon. Bob Majors said Scott would roust him out to play even in freezing temperatures when no one else was on the course. When playing golf, Scott always chewed Red Man tobacco. "You would not want to be downwind," said Majors.

He visited regularly with his son R.K. and granddaughters, Elizabeth Ann and Kathryn Kay. He would drive to their home, first in Omaha and later, after they moved to Denver. Posthumously, Scotty has four grandsons. Scott played cupid and introduced R.K. to his current wife, Susan, arranging a golf outing on the Solon course.

Coach Paul Scott (left) with his greatest wrestler, Lowell Lange circa 1950.

He continued to watch football, always without the sound, saying the announcers were "idiots." He also continued to indulge his enthusiasm for Dixieland jazz, which he had picked up when he was a student at Columbia, and he enjoyed Louis L'Amour novels, each of which he had read at least twice. An international traveler, he took a trip to China as part of a Cornell group when he was in his 90s.

Many of his "boys" would return to visit, and some would play golf. Dale Thomas said, "Scotty made me think of the wrestling team as a family. He was the principal mentor in my life. I play golf with him every time I come to town. Whenever we get together, it's like we've never been apart." In his own coaching career, Thomas was greatly influenced by Scott; as head coach at Oregon State University, he won more dual meets than any other coach in collegiate wrestling history.

There were many homecomings and reunions. One event took place in conjunction with the NCAA championship at the University of Iowa in 1986. Many of Scott's 1947 team were there. Baron Bremner, vice president for development at Cornell and a former Cornell College wrestling coach, was the master of ceremonies, and "Rick" Meredith reminisced, as he always did. Another event was held the following year at Cornell, billed as "An Evening of Toasting and Roasting Scotty on the Occasion of his 82nd Birthday." This time, Rick Meredith was the master of ceremonies.

Paul Scott was inducted into the National Wrestling Hall of Fame in Stillwater, Oklahoma, in the spring of 1992, after a successful campaign led by Bremner. Scott was the last of his contemporaries to be inducted, preceded by two of his own wrestlers, Dale Thomas and Lowell Lange. Mike Chapman, who was a member of the selection committee for several years, believes that the reason for Scott's late induction was his relatively short coaching career (he coached at the college level for only six years). Most of the other great coaches inducted into the Hall had more than 10 years of college coaching experience, and many of them had coached for 20, 30, or even 40 years.

Bob Dellinger, director of the Hall of Fame and noted wrestling historian, said, "Paul's principal achievement was leading a small, private school to two national championships. Operating without recruiting and big athletic scholarships, it's almost unheard of for such a school as Cornell to compete with the likes of Oklahoma State and Iowa State."

The biggest celebration of all was reserved for the 50th anniversary of the Dream Team's 1947 championships, held on May 10, 1997. Cornell College hosted a 1947 Dream Team reunion luncheon at the Richard and Norma Small Multi-Sport Center on campus, with longtime NCAA wrestling announcer, the late Ed Aliverti, serving as master of ceremonies and Myron Roderick, the executive director of the National Wrestling Hall of Fame, making the presentation.

The luncheon concluded with the introduction of 91-year-old Paul Scott and the many team members present, including the Lange brothers. Conspicuous by his absence was Richard Hauser, who never returned to Cornell for reunions of any kind. However, he remained close to Scott, and on several occasions he drove from his home in San Diego to visit Scott at his winter home in Arizona.

In Memoriam

Paul Scott passed away on August 22, 2003, at age 97 years, 10 months, in a hospital in Cedar Rapids, Iowa, after a short illness. A memorial service was held for him on September 27, 2003, at King Chapel on the campus of Cornell College. I was privileged to attend.

It was an early Fall day, blustery and overcast, and the church was filled to capacity. It was most fitting that the Eddie Piccard New Orleans jazz band was on stage along with dignitaries Dr. Leslie Garner, president of the College; Terry Gibson '59, vice president to alumni; Richard Small '50, representing the board of trustees; and close friend Dr. Howard Ruppell. Each participant spoke eloquently of Scott's remarkable life.

Clare Boothe Luce once recounted a conversation she had in 1962 in the White House with President Kennedy. She told him that "a great man is one sentence." That is, he can be so well summed up in a single sentence that one can identify the man by what he achieved. So Richard Small had it right when he said that Paul Scott would always be remembered as the architect of one of the greatest sports achievements of all time—leading a small, private school to two national wrestling championships.

Mike Chapman, who probably knew Paul Scott as well as any person connected to the sport, said that he was the finest gentleman he had ever met, an energetic, interesting, and charming human being. He was a great ambassador for the sport of wrestling, the state of Iowa, and Cornell College. He watched every great champion from Earl McCready, who wrestled for Oklahoma State in the first NCAA championship in Ames in 1928 and became the first three-time champion, to Iowa State star Cael Sanderson, the first undefeated, four-time champion, at the NCAA championship in Iowa City in 2001.

At his retirement dinner Scott had said, "I've really had a very interesting and rewarding life. In athletics, I had unusual success as a coach, and this thing [alumni director] has been just right for me. There isn't a town of any size in the country where I don't have a lot of friends as a result of this." He added modestly, "If I've been good for Cornell, it's been doubly good for me."

Scott's enormous contributions to Cornell College were memorialized in October 2009 when the Paul K. Scott Alumni Center at Rood House was dedicated. This college landmark, which had served as a women's residence hall for most of the past 125 years, now houses the Office for Alumni and College Advancement. Richard and Norma Small spearheaded the fundraising campaign to save the building and name it after Scott.

What Became of Them

Paul Scott, for all his focus on and dedication to producing a winning wrestling team, never lost sight of the value of education for his wrestlers. "Most of my kids were pretty good students," he said. "I didn't have any 'rum dumbs.' Good math students and English students. Most of them became educators. Most of them went on and got master's or doctorate degrees, became real good guys in the field of education. Well, I always encouraged them and I talked a lot about the importance of making good grades whether they were interested in education or not." His "kids" did him proud.

Arlo Ellison '47

After graduation Arlo, who had majored in geology, moved to Montana with his wife, Jeanna, to become a rancher. They raised five children. He lives with his wife on the ranch in Stevensville, Montana, and still rides every day.

Wallace W. "Pic" Littell '47

"Pic" Littell graduated with a major in political science and history and a minor in language; he was a member of Phi Beta Kappa. He attended the Russia Institute of Columbia University, receiving his M.A. in 1949. He entered the foreign service that year and had a distinguished career, serving at various posts in Germany, Moscow, Warsaw, Belgrade, East Berlin, Budapest, and of course, Washington DC. He retired in 1983 with the rank of minister-counselor.

Littell passed away on May 28, 2007 at age 85, just weeks before the induction of the Cornell College team into the National Wrestling Hall of Fame. He is survived by his wife, Ilda Hall Littell, and two children.

Gordon "Rick" Meredith '47

After graduation Rick worked for three years as sports editor of the Mason City (Iowa) *Globe Gazette*. He was recalled to Navy duty during the Korean conflict and served two years on the U.S.S. *Mellett* (APA 156), after which he moved to south Florida, where he spent the majority of his career as a realtor. In the mid-60s he co-founded Meredith Realty, Inc., with his wife, Sara. He assisted in recruiting many Florida high school football players for Cornell.

Meredith was a former president of Cornell's Alumni Association and served on the board of trustees from 1986 to 1995, before being named a life trustee. The Gordon Meredith Athletic Complex is named in his honor.

He died March 8, 2006, in West Palm Beach, Florida, at the age of 83, leaving his wife, a son, a stepson, and nine grandchildren.

Robert Soper '47

A pre-med major at Cornell, Bob served in the U. S. Navy Reserve. He went on to receive his M.D. at the University of Iowa, where he was a surgical resident and then a professor and interim head of the department of surgery. He also established the university's division of pediatric surgery. The Soper Chair in Pediatric Surgery, the first endowed chair in the UI department of surgery, honors him and his wife, Hélène '51. The couple, who live in Iowa City, had four children. Although retired, Dr. Soper serves as professor emeritus in surgery.

Dale O. "Whitey" Thomas '47

After Dale graduated from Cornell, he went back to Purdue to get his master's degree in 1948, while helping Claude Reeck with the wrestling program. He continued to compete while working on his Ph.D. at the University of Iowa, winning a total of nine national AAU championships in freestyle and Greco-Roman wrestling. He was on two Olympic teams: freestyle alternate at 191.5 in 1952; and Greco-Roman in Melbourne in 1956, where he placed fifth. He received his doctorate in 1950.

In 1957 he took over the head coaching position at Oregon State, where he became the driving force behind wrestling in the state. With a dual-meet record of 616–192–12, he became the winningest coach in NCAA history. He coached 22 conference team champions, 60 all-Americans, and the runner-up team in the NCAA championships in 1973. He remained at Oregon State for 34 years, retiring in 1990. Paul Scott attended and spoke at a tribute for Thomas in April 1991, in Portland, Oregon. Thomas was inducted into the National Wrestling Hall of Fame in 1980.

He died in 2004 at age 81 and was survived by his longtime companion, Nadine Ritchey, and four children, David, Kenneth, Steven, and Susan Thomas.

Charles V. Voyce '47

After leaving Cornell to enter the military, Voyce received an appointment to the U.S. Naval Academy and then flew B-29's in the Pacific. He returned to Cornell for his senior year. He began a coaching career in Iowa but was recalled to the Air Force during the Korean conflict and chose to remain in the military. He had a distinguished career retiring as Lt. Colonel in 1965. He then worked in a civilian capacity at Vandenberg Air Force Base for the remainder of his career. He died on October 16, 2003 leaving his wife of 59 years, Christine and four children. They lived in Santa Maria, California.

W. Bennett "Ben" Conner, Jr. '48

After leaving Cornell to enter the military for three years, serving in the Army Air Corps he returned to Cornell to earn his degree

After graduation he received a law degree from NYU School of Law.

He rose through the ranks of AMP (now Tyco) in Harrisburg, PA where he was Corporate Vice President and Director of Marketing. (Throughout his life he served on many non-profit boards.) He married Marcia Bacon '47 in 1949. They had three children and lived in Mechanicsburg, Pennsylvania. The spent many years of retirement traveling to far parts of the globe, which culminated in his writing "Exotic Travel: From the Asmat to Africa," a collection of 14 travel adventures. He died April 15, 2007.

Joe Pelisek '48

Joe graduated with a major in physical education and science and received a master's degree from New Mexico Highlands University. He later took post-master's courses at both the University of Iowa and Kansas State. Joe taught and coached wrestling and football at a Cedar Rapids, Iowa, high school for eight years, then moved on to coach football and wrestling at Monmouth College in Monmouth, Illinois, for eight years, competing against Al Partin's team at Knox. His last position was coaching football at Peru State in Peru, Nebraska. Joe and his wife, Anita, had two children and are now retired and living in Lincoln, Nebraska.

John Gregg '49

John was a biology major at Cornell, and after graduation he went to the University of Minnesota, where he earned his doctorate in veterinarian medicine. He returned to Cherokee, Iowa, and practiced at Correctionville for many years. He married his wife Norma in 1974 and is now retired in Cherokee.

Fred Dexter '50

After graduation Fred returned to the military, this time to the U.S. Air Force, where he served as captain until 1959. He received his master's in educational administration from the University of Northern Illinois. He spent his entire career teaching physical education, science, and mathematics, and of course, coaching wrestling. He retired in 1986 and now lives in Harrison, Missouri.

Richard Hauser '50

After graduation, Hauser went to Purdue University, where he completed his master's degree in education and assisted Claude Reeck with the wrestling program. He won another NAAU title in 1953 at 125.5 pounds. He married and moved to the San Diego area to teach in the public schools. He and his wife, Gloria, had a son and a daughter. Although he never returned to campus for any of the team reunions, he stayed in touch with some of his teammates and remained close to Scott. He is retired in California, where he spends his free time sailing.

Kent Lange '50

Lange, who worked for Bankers Life and Casualty for 40 years, organized one of the first youth wrestling programs in the state of Iowa. Married with four sons, the now-retired executive lives in Clinton, Iowa, with his wife, Carolyn, with whom he recently celebrated their 60th wedding anniversary. They both play golf as much as they can, weather permitting. Kent stays in touch with his younger brother Lowell.

Lowell "Tiger" Lange '50

After serving in military intelligence for three years, Lowell helped his father with farming until 1960, when he acquired a ceramics company dealership and moved to Atlanta with his family. He started a wrestling program at Georgia Tech in 1962 that became a varsity sport in 1964. He coached for many years without much support from the university, trying to keep wrestling alive in the Southeastern Conference. He retired in 1993 and lives near Atlanta with his daughter and son-in-law and his three grandchildren. He was inducted into the National Wrestling Hall of Fame in 1981.

Ben McAdams '50

After graduating, Ben received a master's degree in elementary administration. He was a longtime school administrator for the Moline, Illinois, school district. After retiring as superintendent of schools, he served as CEO of Arrowhead Ranch, a full-service facility serving troubled adolescents. Widowed with six children, McAdams is retired and still lives in Moline.

Al Partin '50

Al married Genevieve Callinan in 1948, while they were still in college. ("Gene," who was from Naperville, Illinois, had been recruited to attend Cornell by Scott in 1944.) The couple had three children.

Al became head wresting coach at Nebraska, where he also assisted in football. After four years, he moved to Knox College in Galesburg, Illinois, where he became head wrestling coach; the next year he was appointed to the newly created position of director of physical education. He remained at Knox for 28 years before retiring to Florida.

He and his wife currently reside in Champaign, Illinois, where their son Richard works at the University of Illinois. Al is still actively coaching his grandchildren and others at the middle school nearby.

Richard P. Small '50

After receiving his degree in economics and business administration from Cornell College. After graduation he worked a short time for an independent gasoline marketing firm in Chicago and in 1952 with his brother Robert he founded Checker Oil Company, an oil marketing firm, by leasing an abandoned gas station in Olympic Fields, Illinois. Under his leadership the company grew to several hundred service stations in 18 states, with sales of $500 million. He sold the company to Marathon Petroleum in 1983. In 1984 he became president and majority shareholder of Tri Star Aerospace in Florida. He sold his interest in 1996.

Retiring in 1998, he and his wife, Norma, moved to Tulsa. When the Smalls met, Norma was working as assistant to Paul Scott when he was alumni director, a job she held for 14 years. The Smalls have five children, two of whom attended Cornell.

The Smalls have been the largest benefactors in Cornell College history, contributing more than $25 million, mostly in the form of challenge grants. The Richard and Norma Small Life Sports Center stands as a tribute to the couple. Their most recent initiative was spearheading the drive for funds for the Paul K. Scott Alumni Center, dedicated October 23, 2009. They have also been major contributors to the National Wrestling Hall of Fame in Stillwater, Oklahoma.

Rodger Snook '50

After graduation, Rodger took a job in the Cornell admissions office. Driving home from a recruiting trip in May 1954, he was hit by drunk driver. He survived the accident, but it left him a severely impaired paraplegic. He ultimately took his own life on May 17, 1956, in his hometown of Newton, New Jersey.

Leo A. Thomsen '50

Following graduation, Thomsen taught and coached high school wrestling for two years in Colby, Kansas. His wrestling team won the 1951 Kansas State High School Championship.

From 1952 to 1974, Thomsen worked for Iowa Manufacturing Co., spending five years in Canada and the remainder of the time in Cedar Rapids, Iowa. At the time of his death from testicular cancer on September 13, 1974, Thomsen was sales promotion coordinator for the company. He left behind his wife, Mary, and the couple's five children—Timothy, Barbara, Bill, Mary, and Martha.

Walter "Mouse" Romanowski '51

After his graduation from Cornell, Walter moved to Purdue to work on his master's in education and to assist Claude Reeck with the wrestling program, succeeding his teammate Hauser in that capacity. Each year he dutifully returned to Chicago to check on his selective service status, and each time he was told to continue with his education. After five years he wound up with a Ph.D. in education psychology in 1956. He continued to compete in some tournaments while at Purdue and won the 1953 Greco-Roman NAAU at 147.5 pounds.

He moved to California where he became an educator in the San Diego school system. He and his wife, Pauline, raised five children. He is now retired.

Acknowledgments

This book could not have been written without the cooperation and encouragement of many people, a few of whom need special mention. First, Richard K. Scott, son of Paul K. Scott, who generously provided me with the Scott archives including his oral history, met with me on several occasions, and took countless annoying phone calls. Next, Mike and Bev Chapman, founders of the International Wrestling Institute and Museum, and their associate Kyle Klingman, with whom I met initially when the museum was located in Newton, Iowa, and later when it moved to Waterloo, Iowa, and was renamed the Dan Gable Institute and Museum. (The museum has recently merged with the National Wrestling Hall of Fame in Stillwater, Oklahoma.) Their patience and knowledge, along with the depth of resources at their fingertips, were invaluable. And importantly Jay Hammond, official historian for the National Wrestling Hall of Fame and author of the definitive *History of Collegiate Wrestling*, was a font of information and advice.

In researching this story I was also fortunate to talk to many of the participants in the events it covers. I conducted in-person interviews that took me from Atlanta to San Diego, visiting with Lowell Lange, Kent

Lange, Fred Dexter, Al Partin, Arlo Ellison, Ben McAdams, Bill Nelson, Bob Siddens, Richard Small, Bob Majors, and Walter Romanowski, along with the now-deceased "Pic" Littell and Gerry Leeman.

In addition, Jane Sattelberg, niece of the late Rodger Snook; Bill Thomsen, son of the late Leo Thomsen; and Sarah Meredith, wife of the late Rick Meredith, all graciously shared anecdotes and personal memories, as well as clippings, photos, and mementos.

I am enormously grateful to the people at Cornell College for their support and enthusiasm for this effort, with special thanks to Sarah Slack for her excellent research. Here in my hometown of Boulder, Colorado, thanks go to my friend Rodger Ewy, who scanned all the photographs, and my designer and publishing coordinator, Wis Mollerud Holt, owner, The Design Garage. Thanks to Elizabeth Gold of "To The Point" writing and marketing whose course showed me the way and to Susan Ackerman, owner of VIP Secretarial Service who painstakingly transcribed the Paul K. Scott interviews.

I would like to thank Jay Hammond and Mike Chapman for reading the manuscript and providing their valuable input.

Lastly, the book could not have been written without my life partner, Brenda Niemand, whose encouragement and considerable professional editing skills helped keep the project on track to completion.

Any errors or mistakes occurring in this book are mine and mine alone.

I consider it my great honor to tell this story and to shine a spotlight on the remarkable people and extraordinary feats it celebrates.

Appendix

Cornell College Dual Meets
1946/47 Season
12–0–1

December 14, 1946	Cornell	26	Fort Dodge YMCA	8 Home (Mount Vernon)
December 20	Cornell	33	Ottumwa Naval Air	3 Home
January 11, 1947	Cornell	26	Iowa State	8 Ames, IA
January 15	Cornell	34	Bradley University	0 Peoria, IL
January 24	Cornell	12	Iowa Teachers	12 Cedar Falls, IA
January 31	Cornell	19	University of Illinois	11 Home
February 4	Cornell	36	Lehigh University	0 Bethlehem, PA
February 5	Cornell	27	Army	2 West Point, NY
February 6	Cornell	24	McBurney YMCA	7 New York, NY
February 8	Cornell	23	Ithaca YMCA	13 Ithaca, NY
February 15	Cornell	17	University of Wisconsin	11 Madison, WI
February 21	Cornell	24	Michigan State	6 Home
March 3	Cornell	26	University of Nebraska	4 Home

1946-'47 DUAL MEET INDIVIDUAL RECORDS

	W.	L.	D.	Pts.	Op.	Wins			Losses		
						P.	D.	M.	P.	D.	M.
Ben Conner, Hwt.	1				5				1		
Fred Dexter, 165-Hwt.	12	1		48	3	5	6	1	1		
Arlo Ellison, 136-155	5	1		17	5	1	4		1		
Johnny Gregg, 121	1				5				1		
Dick Hauser, 121, 128	13			59		10	3				
Kent Lange, 155, 165	2	2		6	6		2			2	
Lowell Lange, 136, 145	12			46		4	7	1			
Wallace Littell, 155, 165	2	2	1	8	10		2		1	1	
Ben McAdam, 121	4			16		2	2				
Al Partin, 165-Hwt.	3	5		15	15	3					5
Joe Pelisek, 175-Hwt.	2	3		6	13		2		2	1	
Dale Sherrill, 121	1	1		2	5					1	
Rodger Snook, 145-165	11		1	49	2	7	4				
Bob Soper, 165	1			3			1				
Dale Thomas, 175-Hwt.	3	1	1	13	7	1	2		1		
Leo Thomsen, 128, 136	8	2		34		5	3			2	
Charley Voyce, Hwt.	2			8					1	1	

Legend: W.—wins, L.—losses, D.—draws, Pts.—total points, Op.—opponents' points. Under wins and losses, P.—pins, D.—decisions, and M.—miscellaneous (includes defaults and forfeits).

The Cornellian, *March 7, 1947*

Grand Slam Winners!

N. C. A. A.	NAT'L. A. A. U.
1st Place: Dick Hauser (121)	1st place: Lowell Lange (135)
Lowell Lange (136)	Dale Thomas (175)
2nd Place: Rodger Snook (145)	2nd place: Rodger Snook (145)
	Dick Hauser (121)
3rd Place: Leo Thomsen (128)	4th place: Leo Thomsen (128)
Fred Dexter (165)	
Dale Thomas (175)	Johnny Gregg (115)
	Arlo Ellison (135)
	Kent Lange (155)
Kent Lange (155)	Al Partin (165)
Al Partin (Hwt.)	Fred Dexter (191)

1947 Iowa state A. A. U. championship—First place: Dick Hauser (123), Leo Thomsen (129), Lowell Lange (136), Rodger Snook (145), and Dale Thomas (175). Second place: Johny Gregg (118), Dale Sherrill (123), and Al Partin (Hwt.). Third place: Arlo Ellison (145), Kent Lange (155), and Fred Dexter (165). Fourth place: Bob Conner (112) and Jack Haloupek (Hwt.).

1947 Midwest conference championship—Champions: Johnny Gregg, Dick Hauser, Leo Thomsen, Arlo Ellison, Kent Lange, Ben Conner and Dale Thomas. Second place: Bob Soper.

The Cornellian, *April 18, 1947*

Cornell College Tournaments
1947

March 1	Midwest Conference	Appleton, WI	First Place
March 7–8	Iowa AAU	Home	First Place
March 28–29	NCAA	Champaign, IL	First Place
April 11–12	NAAU	San Francisco, CA	First Place

National Wrestling Hall of Fame
Distinguished Members Who Figure in This Story

LeRoy A. Alitz

Edward G. Aliverti

Lloyd O. Appleton

David B. Arndt

Richard W. Barker

Henry L. Boresch

Glen Brand

Raymond G. Clapp

Fendley A. Collins

Robert E. Dellinger

Richard DiBatista

Edward B. Eichelberger

Finn B. Eriksen

Dan Gable

Edward Clark Gallagher

Art Griffith

Richard H. A. Hutton

Clifford P. Keen

William H. Koll

Lowell W. Lange

Douglas H. Lee

Gerald G. Leeman

Charles W. Mayser

Earl Gray McCready

David H. McCuskey

William J. Nelson

Hugo M. Otopalik

Myron W. Roderick

Paul K. Scott

Billy Sheridan

Robert S. Siddens

William T. Smith

Charles M. Speidel

Dale O. Thomas

William J. Weick

Henry Wittenberg

Keith F. Young

Cornell's 1947 All-Team Roster

Mark Anthony

William G. Barringer

Bufford "jug" Beck

L. Dean Caraway

W. Bennet "Ben"Conner

Walter R. Conner

Walter C. Crow Jr.

Fred Dexter

Arlo Ellison

Franklin Friday

John Gregg

Richard Hauser

Don Hensel

Donald E. Hoffman

Marshall Jones

Roger W. Lahman

Kent Lange

Robert LeBeau

Wallace W. "Pic" Littell

Harry Marshall Jr.

Ben McAdams

Ben O'Dell

Al Partin

Joe Pelisek

Philip Polgreen

Walter Romanowski

Wallace Schneider

Dale Sherrill

Richard Small

Rodger Snook

Robert Soper

Lynn "Bear" Stiles

Dale O. "Whitey" Thomas

Leo Thomsen

Charles Voyce

Ralph Weber

Coach Paul K. Scott

Manager Gordon D. "Rick" Meredith

Sources

Amateur Athletic Union. "Senior National A.A.U. Wrestling Championships Official Program." The Olympic Club, San Francisco, California, April 11–12, 1947.

Chapman, Mike. *Encyclopedia of American Wrestling*. Champaign, Illinois: Leisure Press, 1990.

———. *From Gotch to Gable: A History of Wresting in Iowa*. Iowa City, Iowa: The University of Iowa, 1981.

———. *Legends of the Mat: Stories of 34 of America's Greatest Wrestlers of All Time*. Newton, Iowa: Culture House Books, 2006.

———. "Dream Team of '47: National Champs Never Equaled." *Cornell Report* (summer 1997): 4–11.

Cornell College. *Royal Purple* yearbooks published by the classes of 1947, 1948, 1949, and 1950. Mount Vernon, Iowa: Cornell College.

———. "Dream Team '47 Reunion Luncheon" program. Cornell College, Mount Vernon, Iowa, May 10, 1997.

Dellinger, Bob, and Doris Dellinger. *The Cowboys Ride Again! The History of Wrestling's Dynasty*. Stillwater, Oklahoma: Oklahoma Bylines, Inc., 1994.

Eriksen, Finn B. *Finn B. Eriksen, Dean of Iowa Wrestling: His Life Work and His Writings*. Edited by West High Cowboys of '42, 1991.

Hammond, Jairus K. *The History of Collegiate Wrestling: A Century of Wrestling Excellence*. Stillwater, Oklahoma: National Wrestling Hall of Fame and Museum, 2006.

Heywood, C. William. *Cornell College: A Sesquicentennial History, 1853–2003*. Vol. 1, 1853–1967. Cedar Rapids, Iowa: WDG Publishing, 2004.

Milhauser, Charles J. *1853–2003, Cornell College: 150 Years from A to Z*. Cedar Rapids, Iowa: WDG Publishing, 2003.

National Collegiate Athletic Association. "N.C.A.A. Wrestling Championships (Seventeenth Annual) Official Program." University of Illinois, Champaign-Urbana, Illinois, March 28–29, 1947.

National Wrestling Hall of Fame and Museum. "National Wrestling Hall of Fame and Museum Award Recipients." Stillwater, Oklahoma: National Wrestling Hall of Fame and Museum, 2007.

Olympic Club of San Francisco. *One Hundred Years: The Olympic Club Centennial 1860/1960*. San Francisco: The Olympic Club, 1960.

Sayenga, Donald, Philip O. Badger, Jr., John J. Harmon, Jay Hammond, and Dennis R. Diehl. *"All-New" History of the Eastern Intercollegiate*

Wrestling Association: The First 100 Years—1905-2004. Third Edition, compiled by John J. Harmon and Jairus K. Hammond, 2004.

Scott, Paul K. Interviews by Linda Yanny conducted in four sessions during October and November 2001. CDs of audio recordings used by permission of Richard K. Scott.

Sports: "Wrestling Played Straight." *Life*, 23 February 1948, 93–94.

Thomas, Richard Harlan. *Cornell College: A Sesquicentennial History, 1853–2003*. Vol. 2, 1967–2003. Cedar Rapids, Iowa: WDG Publishing, 2004.

United States Olympic Committee. "1948 U. S. Olympic Team Trials Official Program." Iowa State College, Ames, Iowa, April 29–May 1, 1948.

Westin St. Francis. "The Westin St. Francis: Celebrating a Century of History on Union Square 1904–2004" (pamphlet). San Francisco, California, 2004.

Young, James V. and Arthur F. McClure. *Remembering Their Glory: Sports Heroes of the 1940s*. South Brunswick and New York: A. S. Barnes and Company, 1977.